If you like Leaders in Gear, thank you for recommending it to a friend, posting it on Facebook, tweeting it (#ligbook), blogging about it or just saying nice things about it at social gatherings and family reunions.

For Vivian and Addison.
My favorite leaders.

Copyright © 2010 by Rhett Laubach

Printed in the United States of America
First Edition: April 2010

ISBN 978-1-4507-0919-4

Special thanks to the following people for their support and encouragement in the writing of Leaders in Gear...

Ashley Laubach
Annette Laubach
Jerry Laubach
Lance Laubach
Kelly Barnes
Bill Cordes
Ryan Underwood
Joe Skeen
Katie McConnell
Kent Boggs
Steve Gratz
Christine Hollingsworth
Brett Evans
Josh Bledsoe
Mary Kane
Ben Lastly
Cheryl Zimmerman
Emily Griffin Overocker
Lyn Fiscus
Curtis Childers

RHETT LAUBACH

rhett@yournextspeaker.com
Connect with Rhett on Facebook, Twitter (yns1), or LinkedIn
405.517.7385

Rhett Laubach has presented high-energy, high-impact
leadership presentations for 17 years, in 47 states, the
District of Columbia, the Bahamas and Canada and in front of
1,000,000 audience members. His clients range from NBA
basketball teams to student leadership organizations to
Fortune 500 companies. Rhett is available to present a
keynote, workshop or training at your next event. Contact
him today to get your group's leadership in gear.

RELATED WEB SITES

Leaders in Gear Blog - *leadersingear.blogspot.com*
YourNextSpeaker Site - *www.YourNextSpeaker.com*
Leadership Curriculum - *www.PersonalLeadershipInsight.org*
Speaking Skills Blog - *www.AuthenticityRules.com*
Rhett's Leadership Links - *www.delicious.com/pliblog*

Contents

SECTION 3 – Get Your Presentations in Gear

APPENDIX

Introduction

129,000,000. That is the number of Google search results for the word leadership. 59,575. Amazon has that many books in its library directly related to the topic. These are just two examples of how popular leadership concepts, principles and stories are in the education, corporate, non-profit and government sectors. They also serve as a reminder of how mind-boggling large the library is for individuals seeking material for personal study and/or teaching purposes. It is overwhelming.

Leaders in Gear is designed to simplify this world for you. It is an easily digestible reference guide to three separate, yet connected disciplines: personal leadership, team leadership and presentations. You will want to consume Leaders in Gear in its entirety; highlighting and circling key thoughts and application points as you go. You should also keep coming back to particular chapters for quick refreshers as you strive for excellence in your leadership journey.

I have included a notes area at the end of the three sections, as well as at the back. If you are a leadership teacher, student leader, corporate trainer, etc., utilize these spaces to capture ideas or speaking points inspired by the book. I began my speaking and leadership teaching career almost twenty years ago as an elected student leader in the Oklahoma FFA Association. Leaders in Gear is the exact type of book I needed then and I believe it will serve your leadership growth and development needs for many years to come.

Rhett!

SECTION 1

GET YOURSELF IN GEAR

Get in Leader Gear

1

Big MO

Every useful brush has a canvas to leave its mark.

> *Big MO is the one big idea that is the anchor for each chapter. MO stands for Motor Oil. The leader behavior, trait, skill or talent that is most needed to add grease to your Leader Gear and move the ideas in the chapter forward.*

Nellie Bagley was a leader in waiting her entire life. She had a meek disposition and let everyone push her around. Then her son Jose received a traumatic brain injury fighting for the United States military in Iraq. The government was not taking care of her son like she thought they should and she got her leadership in gear. Four years of working tirelessly resulted in major changes in the way wounded veterans are treated. Much of this needed change can be attributed to Nellie Bagley stepping up and being a leader. She is not perfect, not a single leader is, but her story is a perfect example of what you can make happen when you go from a leader in waiting to a Leader in Gear.

This book is about the many little actions you can do every day to get your leadership into gear. A third is about your personal leadership journey; your emotions, your commitment, your stress, etc. You can't truly lead others until you first lead yourself. A third is about your leadership for others; their drama, their trust, their growth, etc. The final section is all about your presentations and speaking opportunities. Those times when you get to lead in a big way by delivering messages to a few or a few thousand. Leaders in Gear is your guide to creating value for the people and projects in your life.

We begin this journey by looking at the three elements you need to get right to get into Leader Gear in the first place. This book digs down into a multitude of behaviors, strategies and tactics necessary to be a leader who creates real change in self and others. However, the fuel necessary to get them going and keep them going lies in the following three concepts being actively present in your life.

1. Focus on something bigger than yourself. The best way to have the strength, power and dedication to do all the little things to get and stay into Leader Gear is to put your focus on a greater purpose and mission. Ultimately, my purpose for completing this book and communicating my passion, beliefs and leadership strategies is to bring glory to God. My faith teaches that we must be third - God first, others second and self third. Throughout this book, you will find other core principles of my Christian faith: compassion, servanthood, patience, empathy, forgiveness, fellowship, etc. Communicating my faith and keeping my teachings in alignment with how God calls me to live, lifts up His name and hopefully brings Him glory.

This "greater than me" perspective provides fuel when times get tough. Getting into Leader Gear is a daunting task. Staying there is even more demanding. Put and keep your focus on the greater cause, whatever that is for you. It could be your team, customers, core beliefs or faith.

2. True success and joy are bi-products of helping others. Leader Gear calls you to have your focus on your greater purpose and mission first and on others second. The major financial disasters of the late 1990s and early 2000s serve as a clear demonstration of what happens when very smart leaders mess with this order. The executives at Enron, Tyco and WorldCom to the hoards of financial experts and the consultants who created complicated instruments that led to the crash of the U.S. housing market in 2008 all played their role in an enormous and tragic uproar of unapologetic selfish behavior.

The short term financial and social gains of the few led to the financial and emotional pains of many. They were either never taught, never learned or entirely forgot that genuine long-lasting success is found on the other side of putting others before self. This essence of Leader Gear isn't only found in those purely unselfish devotions like volunteering, teaching, working for a non-profit, etc. There are millions of unsung heroes operating in Leader Gear who live and work on Wall Street and Main Street. You should receive personal gain for the blood, sweat and tears you give. Just make sure you aren't receiving this gain by taking it away from your neighbor, co-worker, team member or customer.

3. Every useful brush has a canvas upon which to leave its mark. Getting into Leader Gear requires a reason, a purpose, a place, a team, a project and/or an idea. You reading this book means you more than likely already have one or more of these. They are essential for your leadership to create real change and value. The secret is not that you need a canvas on which to leave your mark. The secret is that you need to whittle down the size of your canvas for your colors to be bright, bold and substantial. Don't try to be everything to everyone. Although this book covers a wide swath of leadership topics, skills and application points, you need to take a different approach. Focus your leadership strongly in one or two areas. As those areas gain color and strength, you can move on to others.

Trying to be everything to everyone is a recipe for disaster. Pick and choose your battles. Prioritize. Think like a master surfer riding a wave. His most important ally is the ability to be totally present; using all his physical and mental strength to read the moment, adjust quickly on the fly and make it to shore safely. Being in Leader Gear means being 100% present for the people and projects that need your time, attention and leadership. On their behalf, thank you for giving 100% to moving from a leader in waiting to a Leader in Gear.

The Leaders in Gear Credo

Leaders in waiting defend their weaknesses.
Leaders in Gear leverage their strengths.

Leaders in waiting see threats.
Leaders in Gear see opportunities.

Leaders in waiting admit nothing.
Leaders in Gear admit mistakes.

Leaders in waiting discuss problems.
Leaders in Gear discuss solutions.

Leaders in waiting make isolated decisions.
Leaders in Gear ask for help.

Leaders in waiting act accidentally.
Leaders in Gear act on purpose.

Leaders in waiting do then think.
Leaders in Gear think then do.

Leaders in waiting listen for the sake of self.
Leader in Gears listen for the sake of others.

Leaders in waiting put results before relationships.
Leaders in Gear put relationships before results.

Leaders in waiting seek to be successful.
Leaders in Gear seek to be significant.

(Poster version available. Email rhett@yournextspeaker.com.)

How Leaders Think

2

Big MO

If you can't be excellent at it, don't be it at all.

The greatest performance gap between leaders in waiting and Leaders in Gear is how they think. This is extremely liberating if you wish to get your leadership in gear because the biggest change you need to make is to change your thinking – something totally within your control.

This book offers concrete answers and strategies to the very ambiguous world of leadership challenges. This concreteness begins by understanding that your effectiveness as a leader is entirely based on your performance. Do you and your team produce the desired results? What change do you cause? How are you, your people and your organization/product/service better because of your work? What more do your students know today than they did yesterday? How are you leading today?

This performance-based measuring stick can be both a gift and a curse. It demands that you measure stuff – output, performance, widgets, profit, test scores, engagement, team dynamics, etc. However, it can also serve as a blinder and trump the more subtle forces at work that ultimately help you achieve your goals – your body language, your team's well-being, your stress level, the customer's opinion and more.

Ultimately though, leaders are called to think differently and about different things than everyone else. Your leadership is going to be served best by following these three strategies thinking leaders use to change the world. They think about their personal performance in three specific ways:

If you can't be excellent at it, don't be it at all. Excellence can be reached in most any endeavor with enough hard work. If you aren't willing to put in the elbow grease necessary to reach excellence, then find something else you are willing to give your best to. This is an especially critical principle for leaders because your behavior influences the behavior of many others. This is a responsibility not to be taken lightly. It can seem like a burden at times, but that is why you are in your position and not someone else – because you are expected to carry the load.

If you aren't failing, you aren't pursuing excellence. If you aren't learning from your failures, you will never be excellent and you should re-read number one. I heard someone once say, "I learn so much from my failures, I think I will have some more of them." They were just joking around of course, but the lesson remains. Once you truly engage your leadership, you will fall down, your answers will not always be right and you will make mistakes. This is your leadership going through growing pains, maturing and providing you with priceless learning moments. My great friend, mentor and speaking peer Bill Cordes calls these "Great Moments." If you aren't having them, you aren't pursuing excellence.

If you aren't excellent today, there is a reason. Something needs to change, improve, or stopped. Finding out what that something is requires a heroic level of self-awareness. One of the big goals of Leaders in Gear is to challenge, stretch and mold you into a leader with few blind spots, many bright spots and equipped to change the lives of others through leadership.

An example of how this difference in thinking can change leadership is how highly effective student leaders operate. Many student leaders only engage their leadership during events, meetings and other required duties. Highly effective student leaders who strive for excellence in leadership do things a little differently. Instead of taking this fire hose, either totally on or totally off approach, they do little things every day to maximize the impact they can make during their short-lived one or two years of elected service. They write emails and letters, make phone calls, do chapter visits and seek out other small, but powerful opportunities to connect with their members, advisers, business partners and volunteers.

If you are an elected student leader, follow these guidelines for knowing which of your actions fall into the "above and beyond the call of duty" category:

1. *Encouraged, but not required.*
2. *Not tied to an event.*
3. *Does not require someone else to take action.*
4. *You enjoy doing it.*
5. *You have to sacrifice something to make it happen.*
6. *Not something you currently do on a regular basis.*
7. *Makes a positive difference in the lives of others.*

Avoid Entitlement

3

Big MO

High performers are in love with their craft.

Who do you think of when you think of a wildly successful person? Sports star? Movie star? Personal hero? Whoever you think of, why are these individuals so good at what they do? Are they born with special talents? Is it all hard work? Is it part luck and part something else? Are these characteristics mainly skills, talents, or attitudes?

Chances are your big performers have very different reasons why they are successful and chances are almost as good those success attributes fall under different categories. The lesson here is that the full reasons why and how successful people are so successful seem to be unique depending on the person and their journey to the top.

However, most big performers do have two very important traits in common.

1. Regardless of industry, position, personality, market conditions, expertise, training, talent, skill or attitude, big performers are willing to do the small, non-sexy, gritty, "down in the trenches" tasks the average or under performers either don't want to do or don't think they should have to do. Big performers are in a never-ending battle with entitlement. They are in love with their craft and doing it, not all the perks that come along with being great. A Dutch psychologist studied the difference between chess masters and grand chess masters.

He found it had nothing to do with IQ, memory or skill. The difference between good and great was love. The grand chess masters had more love and commitment to the game.

2. Big performers don't see themselves as big performers. They see themselves as growing performers. They are constantly getting better, learning, stretching, risking, pursuing and running. Big performers are in a never-ending battle with complacency. They seek out growth opportunities by attending conferences, reading books, subscribing to blogs, seeking out mastermind groups, learning from a mentor and self-evaluating.

Healthy Stress

Big MO

Keeping fuel tanks full protects healthy stress.

Stress is consuming my life… I wish I could enjoy life, but I am too stressed out to enjoy anything… My stress level would go down tremendously if I could only get a raise at work… If my husband and kids were more understanding, I wouldn't be so stressed out…

These are the normal, everyday words of millions of Americans going through life in a state of imbalance. They have developed the habit of letting circumstances, situations, and people control their moods, attitudes, and stress levels. Consequently, they feel out of control, out of time, and out of energy. In reality, what they really are experiencing is living out of balance. This imbalance turns healthy stress into destructive distress. Stress is a healthy thing in a balanced life. It challenges us, drives us, and helps to keep our leadership in gear. However, this fuel can easily and quickly turn lethal when we live an imbalanced life.

There are four primary fuel tanks in the human body – physical, mental, emotional and spiritual. These are the wells where we draw the energy to keep healthy stress from turning into destructive distress. Therefore, it is not our time, our checkbook, or even our stress level that needs balancing. We must continually keep our energy in balance by refilling, repairing, and re-engaging our four fuel tanks.

When we let even one of these wells dry up or become damaged, it dramatically impacts our ability to keep healthy stress from turning into destructive distress. This imbalance prohibits us from getting, storing, or engaging the energy we need to operate at effective levels. It is also important to understand the four centers operate interdependently. They are very much like the pistons in our cars. When one is not firing properly, the engine will continue to run, but it will not run effectively, efficiently, or smoothly. Additionally, it will not run for very long in that continued state of imbalance and will eventually breakdown all together.

How do we know when our healthy stress has evolved into destructive distress? A very evident signal is when someone else's thoughts, words, and actions drastically affect our behavior. Doing this essentially hands control over to that person or situation. The biggest reason for this common pattern is it allows us to dodge responsibility. If I can blame someone or something for my problems, then I don't have to accept personal responsibility for creating or advancing deficiencies in one, many, or all of my fuel tanks.

The first step in achieving balance is to accept and hold a firm commitment to the fact that we are exactly where we have chosen to be, we think exactly what we choose to think, we act exactly how we choose to act, and our energy level is exactly where we choose it to be. This first step is a tremendously difficult and, at the same time, liberating act of accepting personal responsibility for our thoughts, words, actions and emotions.

I had a friend who, while in college, stayed under extreme distress even though she had very little going on in her life outside of class – no activities, no clubs, no job, and no hobbies. Even with all this extra time on her hands, her grades suffered and she was miserable. She became paralyzed by destructive distress because she had chosen not to accept the fact that she had created the situation or to truly believe she could do anything about it. She felt out of control and she blamed her situation on homesickness, on the university for not providing enough opportunities (there were over 300 clubs on campus), and various outside factors. Her healthy stress had turned into destructive distress because she had handed control over to other people. Additionally, her ability to regain control was damaged because she had allowed her fuel tanks to deplete.

How do we discipline ourselves to take personal responsibility on a daily basis? The second step is to approach our daily lives with a firm belief in the dynamics of true optimism. The best definition of optimism I have heard says, "Recognize your challenges, but work on solutions; understand your weaknesses, but capitalize on your strengths; have many reasons to complain and choose not to."

An example is another friend who had more than her share of job responsibilities, home duties and extracurricular stuff going on in her life. She was under tremendous distress due to her inability and unwillingness to effectively organize and manage her energy. At the heart of her dilemma, however, was her habitual nature to focus on the negative, relish in talking about her weaknesses and complaining. Her situation is a perfect example of how a lack of optimism paralyzes our ability to keep healthy stress from turning into destructive distress. Even if she organized her time or did away with some of her responsibilities, she still would not have enough energy to be effective. Why? Because she was choosing to react negatively to life, instead of responding positively to it.

The third step in achieving balance is to understand that we will never be able to fully handle stress. We can only choose how we are going to respond to the situations that turn healthy stress into destructive distress. It is a simple act of choosing to respond, not react, to what happens to us. Responding is a tool that allows us to make a conscience decision on how we are going to deal with life. Reacting is an "in the heat of the moment" method that many times damages our ability to keep healthy stress from turning into destructive distress.

These three steps are active methods of producing the foundation for addressing stress with success. This foundation, combined with the constant attention to refilling, repairing and re-engaging our four fuel tanks, will ensure a life filled with healthy stress.

Get & Stay Happy

5

Big MO

Give praise, build others and serve the greater good.

What is the driving force of your happiness? When your Life Instantly Feels Tremendous, why? What gives your life LIFT?

It's important to notice the emotion in question here is happiness, not joy. Think of happiness as short bursts of energy that are powerful, fleeting and created by good things that happen in life. Joy is just as powerful, but is a more sustained state that sticks around no matter what is going on in life. However, joy gains energy from moments of happiness and helps you survive the bad times. We all know people who get happy from time to time, but who are missing joy in their life. They live on a roller coaster and have little to no consistency in their emotional life. These individuals need to figure out how to have more happiness in their life and to understand that happiness is shallow without a foundation of joy.

What creates happiness in your life? More importantly, as a leader, is your LIFT created primarily by giving or receiving? I.e. when you think about your good times, are they a result of people or circumstances lifting you up or you lifting others? The most effective leaders and managers focus their LIFT on giving praise, building others, and serving the greater good.

The concept of LIFT in terms of achieving happiness is comparable to the lift that creates flight for airplanes in four specific ways. Examining each might give you some insight into how to have more moments of happiness throughout your day. This will result in strengthening your leadership abilities because the fuel of life is a positive attitude mixed with helping others achieve a positive mindset, as well.

1. It is an intentional act. It takes a coordinated effort of many different people and machines to get an airplane into the air. There are times when we get happiness from unexpected people and places, but consistent happiness is drawn from the pool of taking intentional steps to respond positively to life's circumstances. Happy people do not have great days consistently. They respond positively to the days they have consistently.

2. It takes a good amount of energy to create it. The best example of this in flight is the space shuttle. The amount of energy it takes to pull that massive airplane from the earth's gravitational pull is enormous. Those booster rockets have to work hard to make it happen. Happiness also takes hard work. It doesn't take much effort to be sad, negative or pessimistic. It does take time and effort to make happiness a regular visitor in your life. It is easier for some more than others. Each of us has a default demeanor that was formed early in life. Yet, another reminder that we are mostly hard wired by the age of six. Development after that age is software upgrades. The happiness upgrade requires a large amount of resources, but it is well worth it.

3. People see it, but mostly don't understand it. Line up ten non-rocket scientists and you will be lucky to get one correct answer of how lift works in aerodynamics. Happiness is elusive to many people; at least genuine happiness is. Genuine happiness is the kind that isn't followed by negative baggage. I.e. when you seek out happiness from putting things into (alcohol/drugs) or doing things to your body (plastic surgery), you might have a surge of good feelings in the short term, but in the long term these actions result in guilt or shame. Many people don't grasp the concept of how to create genuine happiness because they are blinded by the hard work it requires and because many times it involves being entirely others-focused.

Genuine happiness can be very counter-intuitive. A great example is parenting. Many parents feel unhappy in their role because they are looking inward instead of outward. Parenting is tough and tiring. The genuine happiness comes from focusing on the end result of your work; happy, well-adjusted and caring children.

4. Once it is created there are large forces fighting it.
Gravity is the most pervasive force on earth. You cannot escape it. Gravity is constantly working against lift. There are multiple forces working against your happiness. The primary one is other people who do not have it. They would give anything to have your genuine happiness and many times they can only create it in the short term by putting down or making fun of yours. These people can and will diminish your happiness if you let them. However, as a skilled leader, your task is to understand these forces, work hard to fight back, be human and admit when you can't and keep a smile on your face and love in your heart through as much of it as possible.

Commit

6

Big MO

People give their time to what is really important to them.

Getting people to follow you is a matter of trust. This trust has its foundation in your ability to keep your commitments. The most enduring example of commitment breaking creating havoc is in the home. When married couples decide to break their commitment to each other or a parent decides to break their commitments, whether small or large, to their children, it leaves a long trail of heartbreak, insecurity and pain. The number one way to reduce crime in America is to teach men to be better men of character for their children – especially their young boys. The majority of all crimes are committed by males and most major criminals did not have a stable home life or a positive male role model in their life.

Getting your leadership in gear starts with getting your ability to make and keep commitments.

1. Know when to say no. Base your decisions on a few basic questions. Do I have time to do this with excellence? Am I the best person to do this? Do I have the skills and talent? Is now the best time for me to commit to this?

2. Stick to a list of priorities. This requires a heroic level of self-awareness and then discipline to follow through. However, once you have your major priorities and smaller daily ones clearly identified, it will clarify your commitment moves.

3. Under-promise and over-deliver. Be realistic when making promises almost to the point of being your own devil's advocate. Then be unexpectedly optimistic when delivering on your commitments.

4. Gain clarity on all time and duty expectations. Many moments of broken trust come from wishy-washy expectations. Be clear up front on as many commitment points as possible.

5. Apologize quickly. All busy, successful leaders fall from time to time. Meetings are missed. Deadlines are forgotten. Trust is broken. Be quick to apologize and do it in person.

6. Repeated behavior hurts the most. Because everyone falls from time to time, most once or twice mess-ups can be forgiven. The warning flag is thrown up when commitments are broken over and over again.

7. Show up early. One of the simplest ways to build trust with others is to respect their time and attention. Don't ask them to commit to useless tasks or projects and don't be late to the valuable ones.

8. You make time for the important things. You can easily tell what is important to someone – they give it their time. When you give your time and attention to those you lead, you are subtly lifting their sense of importance and value.

9. If you add a commitment, take one away. Unless you have a ton of disposable time, your calendar is just like a full cup. If you put more liquid in, something has to come out. Never take on a new commitment without also committing to stop doing something else.

Grow

7

Big MO

Challenging goals are growth food.

Any high performer knows they reach a point where they have to make a commitment move to inspire their performance to the next level. My friend and serial entrepreneur Stewart Kennedy tells the story of a rock climber who has seemingly climbed as high as he could. He has reached a point where the next hand hold is just out of reach. To go higher he has to literally let go of where he is and leap for the next hand hold. This leap is called a commitment move.

This is a great example of the first step high performers must make to inspire their personal performance. They must take a risk. Ask yourself, "In what ways have I been playing it safe as a leader?" Your answers to this question might include conversations you haven't had, opportunities you haven't pursued or projects you haven't started. A commitment move isn't easy. In fact it's scary. However, it is necessary for you to grow.

The commitment move is also a metaphor for step two, which is aiming for something. You might be in a similar predicament in your personal or professional life today. You are enjoying some success, things are going well and you might be getting comfortable. It is more than likely time to aim for something new and more challenging. What you need is a project, idea, or proposition that truly inspires you –

something worthy of your time, attention and best effort. You need a new goal.

Step three is to leverage your relationships to get there. Life is a team sport. Things get done through people, not systems or emails or silos. If you are struggling to reach a higher level, start connecting with people who are at or near that level already. Learn from them. Lean on them. Find a way to help them. If the relationship is authentic, they will learn, lean and help back. It is also extremely important to seek out feedback from key people in your life. When you get your leadership in gear, you earn more responsibility, titles, influence and power. This can create a one-way transfer of information from you to others because you are in charge and others around you aren't officially in a position to offer you constructive criticisms. Purposefully seek feedback from people you trust. Ask them to hold you accountable to your goals, values and beliefs.

The final step is to examine where your energies are directed. Energy is one of those unique resources that is not finite like time or money. Energy comes from the weirdest and sometimes most unexpected sources. If you need to go to the next level, you will need to redirect your energies to new places and you will need to create energy from new sources – new relationships, new clients, new books, new interests, etc. This is not easy, but it is attainable. The toughest thing about energy in the context of reaching higher is how much it takes to get there. As a high performer, you are more than likely on auto-pilot in a number of areas. This auto-pilot has to be disengaged and you must take over the wheel again.

It is exhausting, but if you are fully committed to taking the risk, if your "something" is worth the aim and if the relationships are leveraged properly, you will be creating more energy than you expend. Someone in your immediate circle and an infinite number of people in new circles need you to go there.

Wired for Success

8

Big MO

Push the boundaries.

What does it take to reach success in any field? It entirely depends - if you are trying to fully explain each high-achiever's individual success. The most common traits that show up on these lists include determination, luck, hard-work, timing, passion, intelligence, networking, etc. However, upon closer examination you will find there is a common thread. It is called the Threshold Thread.

The Threshold Thread concept states that all high achievers have developed the ability to push their capacities further than the average person. Their threshold for hard work is higher. Their patience threshold is longer. Their commitment threshold is stronger. Will Smith has been quoted as saying that the true secret to his success is an insane work ethic. He uses running as an example. If you were on a treadmill beside him he knows one thing for certain - you will get off first.

Will Smith and other inspirational leaders are wired for success through years of hard work, focus and perseverance. Some of their success can be traced to genetics and other "right place at the right time" elements. But most of their wiring was hand placed. You have to ask yourself, "In what areas do I need to push the boundaries a little more to be a better leader?" The answers to this question might be the start of your next gearing up for leadership project. Just remember – don't get off the treadmill first.

Find the Time

9

Big MO

Make time for Epic Journeys.

Merlin Mann, founder and writer of the popular blog 43 Folders, a blog about finding the time and attention to do your best work, did a talk at Google titled Inbox Zero. It is about the benefits of attaining and maintaining an empty email inbox. In the talk he compared our time to a box full of really cool stuff. If we put something lousy in, there won't be room for great things. Therefore, if we are truly committed to creating cool stuff (like getting our leadership in gear), we should be acutely concerned with keeping lousy stuff out of our box. One of the major differences between successful and unsuccessful leaders is their ability to do just that.

You might already think you are doing a good job of this. You are getting things done, surviving the days and haven't gone insane yet. However, let's look at six indicators of good time management and see how you are doing.

1. You get an adequate amount of sleep. Success in multiple fields is based on energy. This means you need fuel. There are many different types of fuel: healthy food, emotional support, intellectual stimulation, professional development, etc. The most important fuel is sleep. Some people can function at a high-level with five hours of sleep and some need eight hours. You need to figure out what your optimal sleep number is and work to get it as often as possible.

2. You meet deadlines. Leadership is based on trust. One of the best ways to build and maintain trust with others is to only say yes to those deadlines you can deliver and then deliver on time or early. This consistency for earliness can only be achieved by managing your time.

3. You are working on meaningful projects. This is a vital indication of someone who manages their time. If you are able to have time to work on meaningful projects, it means you have found a way to minimize the time you have to invest on trivial projects. Not an easy task, but critical to great leadership.

4. You have the right type of stress. Losing weight, achieving wealth and reducing stress are three of the most popular themes of late night infomercials. Coincidentally, two of them are counter-productive. Having a ton of money doesn't make your life simpler, easier or full of sleep-filled nights. Ask your average multi-millionaire or your lucky lottery winner if they have more stress or less stress now compared to their pre-money days and chances are each dollar brought more stress. The trick is not to reduce stress, but to have the right type of stress. The right type of stress is created by challenging life tasks you have chosen to work on - marriage to the love of your life, children, doing what you love at work, challenging hobbies, etc. These activities all create stress, but stress that is wanted and necessary for growth and creating value in life.

5. You follow the rules. Good time managers don't have to cut corners to meet deadlines. They don't have to skip breakfast, drive too fast, be short with people, under-deliver on a project, etc. The basic rules of successful living exist, are well-known and are achievable if you manage your time instead of letting your time manage you.

6. You have time for your Epic Journeys. All of us have those big life missions, wish list items, etc. These are Epic Journeys. They are the things that make it into people's Bucket Lists - "must do before I die" activities. Your average person (i.e. - not retired, super wealthy, jobless, or a college student) who has time for their Epic Journeys has that time because of many factors. The biggest one is their ability to manage their time in such a way to make room in their life for their Epic Journeys.

EPIC JOURNEYS

- Travel overseas
- Volunteer at a homeless shelter or soup kitchen
- Do stand-up comedy
- Run a marathon
- Write a book
- 30 uninterrupted minutes every day with children
- Learn a new hobby
- Learn a foreign language
- Take a week-long vacation with your parents
- Fly in a blimp
- Visit all the seven wonders of the world
- Spend New Years in New York City
- Visit Mardi Gras in New Orleans
- See the Cherry Blossoms bloom in Washington DC
- Mentor a young boy or girl

- Visit the Louvre in Paris
- Shake Mickey's hand at Disneyland
- Ride the ten largest roller coasters
- Take a four-day road trip with no destination in mind
- Go to lunch every Wednesday with your family
-
-
-
-
-
-

Stay Honest

10

Big MO

Attach a strong positive anchor to the truth.

Getting your leadership in gear requires more responsibilities and higher stakes. You know you need to be honest, but do you know how to remain honest while having to deal with high level pressure?

We aren't always honest because of self-preservation, relationship-preservation, the truth will lead to a difficult conversation, we can't remember what the truth is or we will lose something important to us. The real challenge here is not identifying the items on this list, the real challenge is recognizing the reason for the dishonesty in the moment and figuring out how to stop trading our trust with others for these reasons. The reasons we are dishonest cut to the core. We deeply want to protect ourselves and our relationships. We want to avoid conflict with others at all costs. This only adds to the difficulty of mastering the honesty equation. There are many compelling reasons to lie. Your task is to locate and focus on all the reasons to be honest.

Leaders in Gear fight this fight every day in a big way. They are very self-aware of their core beliefs and values and they behave accordingly. The solution to the honesty equation is complicated and varied. Start with attaching a strong positive anchor to telling the truth. Dishonesty produces a tremendous amount of unnecessary stress in our lives. Continually remind yourself the short-term stress of honesty is tiny when compared to the overwhelming weight of lies stacked on lies.

Get to the truth as quickly as possible. A small white lie can turn into a major black hole when days and weeks are added into the equation. Finally, remind yourself of all the great leaders who handicapped their ability to create value and change because they fell into the trap of dishonesty. Leaders in Gear are greatly interested in creating long-term change and leaving a legacy. These purposes are very difficult to create after indiscretions topple your house of trust. Remind yourself of that the next time you are faced with a decision.

Create Cool Stuff

11

Big MO

Cool ideas are made from elbow grease.

Weekend Edition is a skit on Saturday Night Live. The process that the writers go through to create the jokes that make it on the short bit teaches a quick lesson on finding creative ideas and solutions. Each week, the three main SNL writers create eight-hundred jokes for Weekend Edition. The head writer for SNL then whittles that list down to two-hundred that they think are Weekend Edition worthy. Lorne Michaels, the head boss at SNL, then chops that down to twenty jokes that actually make the cut. To get to twenty working lines, they have to come up with forty times that many.

The next time you either think you can't find an answer or need a more creative idea, look a little closer, go a little deeper, and work a little harder. Sometimes cool ideas come to you in a flash of white light. However, most of the time they start with a flash, but are ultimately a product of tons of elbow grease.

Once a great idea is generated in a team environment, then the leadership really matters. Nothing kills a great idea faster than sending it to a committee that isn't prepared to deal with it.

I once facilitated a six-hour brainstorming session with the student organization leaders of a Missouri high school. Our purpose was to develop a community service project that all the organizations could work on together. After four hours the students voted to re-model and re-open their run down city park. Two seconds after the vote was cast, the committee started breaking down and killing the idea with negative talk. "We've tried this before. We will never get this accomplished while we are in high school. There are too many local and state regulations. The city will never cooperate."

The next hour was filled with a crystal clear picture of what really kills or energizes the enthusiasm in ideas and people - disapprovers and improvers. The students focusing only on the negatives and the reasons why the idea was bad were acting as disapprovers. Those students who chose to view the negatives as challenges and focus more on the positives were acting as improvers. With a little persistence and some good leadership, the improvers outweighed the disapprovers and the disapprovers agreed to get behind the idea and work together to accomplish the common goal. The students were left with two thoughts:

1. The park idea is a good or a bad one based largely on whether they think it is good or bad. Their approach in thinking about the situation defines the situation. As the leader of your team, you must help shape and possibly define the way they look at the ideas they are working on. They need your inspired thinking to see the potential in the idea and to believe in their ability to make it a reality.

2. The quality of their effort as a school in completing the project will be determined by how effectively the disapprovers can get as passionately behind the idea as they were able to get so passionately against it. After a decision is made with your team, your major roles are diplomacy and encouragement. Most importantly, when a decision is made you do not totally agree with it, make the good choice to agree to disagree and choose to be an improver and get behind it one-hundred percent.

On September 17, 1787, the final day of the Constitutional Convention, Pennsylvania delegate Benjamin Franklin modeled this lesson. Although he was too weak to deliver the speech (fellow Pennsylvanian James Wilson delivered it for him), the power of his words cannot be overstated. He essentially said that he believed the Constitution to be incomplete and filled with errors. However, it was time for all the men in that room to sign it and then go back to their people and stand up for everything right in it and not focus on what was wrong with it. He said he didn't believe in everything in the instrument, but he did whole-heartedly believe in the process in which the instrument was made.

> *"I doubt too whether any other Convention we can obtain, may be able to make a better Constitution. For when you assemble a number of men to have the advantage of their joint wisdom, you inevitably assemble with those men, all their prejudices, their passions, their errors of opinions, their local interests and their selfish views. From such an assembly can a perfect production be expected? It therefore astonishes me, Sir, to find this system approaching so near to perfection as it does... the opinions I have had of its errors, I sacrifice to the public good... within these walls they were born, and here they shall die."*
> *Benjamin Franklin, Constitutional Convention*

Personal skills also come to play as leaders create cool stuff. There are four personal attributes of consistently creative people.

1. Fluency. When posed with a question, situation, challenge or problem, the consistently creative leader seeks out and tries on tons of potential answers. This reinforces the message behind the magic of the SNL writer's room. Great ideas hide under piles of hard work, bad ideas and self-doubt. They are picky and even elitists – only wanting to reveal themselves to those who deserve to see them.

2. Flexibility. The consistently creative leader not only thinks out of the box, but attempts to color the box, turn the box into an airplane, finds the box maker, studies the history of boxes, gets back in the box and then back out, etc. You need to approach the challenge from a different person's viewpoint; put yourself in their shoes. What would they highlight, expand, contract, delete, replace or magnify?

3. Awareness. There are very few problems you will face that are brand, spanking new. The creation of something new requires an examination and appreciation of that which is old. It is almost a guarantee that someone, somewhere has tried to work on a problem similar to yours. There is also a very good chance someone took the time to write down their solutions in a book, magazine article, website or blog. Getting more creative many times starts with getting more connected and aware.

4. Originality. This may seem like a no brainer, but it is actually exactly the opposite. Your grey matter is totally unique from every other person on earth – 1 in 6 billion. No one has experienced, read, seen, heard, spoken, felt, smelled or touched exactly what you have. That means that you have the opportunity to create authentic output. Don't be afraid to do it. Exercise that muscle often and it will be one of your greatest strengths. The path to exercising your innate ability to be creative and make cool stuff has many barriers. They exist as a filter to weed out those leaders who aren't willing to put in the time, attention or hard work necessary to uncover the best ideas out there. These barriers have less to do with you and more to do with the process. They are a reality for most people trying to create cool stuff. Here are three you will need to work to overcome.

Barrier #1 – Fear of Failure. This one drives the other two and by itself is a creativity killer. The bigger discussion is identifying the true source of this fear. Is it pride? Is it job security? Is it past experiences? Is it saving face? More than likely it is a combination of all. However, the truth is if you overcome these issues, you will surprise yourself by your creative output. Some ideas for overcoming barrier number one: laugh at yourself, kick up your fluency, deliver quickly, and don't tie your self-worth to your job title, status or performance. Your value is not equal to the value of your ideas. You have worth even if you are currently creating crummy solutions. It's not the end of the world if your idea factory is a little under the weather right now. Push through the fear, employ the right strategies and you will find the value of your ideas will begin matching the value of you.

Barrier #2 – It's not my job. The lack of personal responsibility rears its ugly head everywhere, especially in leadership circles. Many positional leaders lifted to their current status because of a mixture of taking responsibility (more than likely on things that no one else wanted to do) and of dodging personal responsibility (in order to protect what they have built – career, project, friendship, etc.) It is amazing what gets created that wasn't there before because someone said, "That's not my job, but I will take care of it." If you are officially leading a team, chances are good this behavior trait is one you value highly in your team members. Model it for them and do more than you are expected to do; both at and below your current pay grade.

Barrier #3 – I'm Not Creative. There is an insightful 18-minute TED keynote delivered by Sir Ken Robinson in 2006. He spoke about the dynamic in schools around the globe where the system is robbing our children of their creativity and imagination capacities by teaching students from the neck up and slightly to the right. This is to say that it shouldn't be a surprise that you or your team are not comfortable being creative or have a self-perception of not being creative. From early in your life, you have been taught to color in the lines, memorize the correct answers, sit still, etc. All of which are important for creating clones and horrible at encouraging and fostering your ability to create cool stuff. You are creative. You need to rediscover the imagination you used every day when you were five, dust off the cobwebs and start getting utility out of it again.

Solve Problems

12

Big MO

Focus on the cause, not the conditions.

Albert Einstein was asked how he would save the world in one hour. He said he would spend fifty-five minutes defining the problem and five minutes solving it. This quote illustrates the importance of having a clear understanding of your problem's core.

Leaders in Gear understand the importance of correctly identifying the cause of problems. I do an activity with my audiences called Balloon Toss that clearly demonstrates this principle. The object of the leadership experiment is for a team of six to eight individuals to keep ten to fifteen balloons in the air and in motion at the same time. The balloons are fed to the team one at a time, the balloons can't be tied together and the team members must keep one hand behind their back the entire time. After the first round of competition is over, we discuss how to improve their chances of success during the second round. I begin this by discussing possible answers to the question, "What was the main reason you were not able to accomplish your goal?"

The leaders normally begin to list conditions, instead of causes. The say things like too many balloons, we could only use one hand, we didn't have a good plan, etc. These are true, but most of their answers are unchangeable conditions within the constraints of the activity - like most of the conditions you are faced with every day. Once the leaders get bogged down in discussing conditions, they handicap their ability to recognize a cause or make any real improvement in their strategy for round two.

The primary cause for not achieving their goal of getting all balloons in the air at once was that the balloons were out of control. Once the leaders recognized this primary cause they were better able to creatively discover the best strategy for getting all balloons in the air at once.

This dynamic happens in every boardroom, classroom and factory. When faced with a problem, it is all too easy to start pointing fingers, wishing for the unattainable or blaming the problem on conditions. Your job as a leader is to step back and look at where you and your team have your focus - is it on unchangeable conditions or solvable causes? Have you driven down to the core of the challenge or are you still playing around on the safe and obvious surface? It is only after discovering a problem's root cause can you begin to create a solution with a fighting chance.

How Leaders Fail

13

Big MO

Success is determined by what you do with failure.

My good friend Curtis Childers was very successful throughout his youth. His success ultimately led to his election to national president of the National FFA - a youth organization with over 500,000 members. After that term, Curtis was elected as student body president of Texas A&M - a major university with over 40,000 students. His highs in life were equaled only by his lows in life. A ten year battle with addiction ended in near death accident that resulted in him struggling to learn how to talk and walk all over again. Although he lost many things throughout his addiction and accident, one thing he didn't lose was his ability to set his mind and purpose on a goal and make that goal a reality.

Curt's goals might be different now, but his ability to dedicate his resources to them is not. His determination, partnered with his positive outlook and joyous spirit, has taken him from a hospital bed with doctors recommending his family to take him off of life support (they thought his brain would never recover enough to even be able to talk or respond to others) to making plans to hit the speaker's circuit to share his story with others. He says before his accident he knew everything there was to know about speaking, but had no story to tell and now he has a story to tell, but has to learn how to speak again. Curtis is a shining example that success in life does not come down to whether or not you experience failure, but how you respond to it.

Failure is a reality of life for all of us. None of us achieve what we want all the time. Leaders do not have less failure than other people. They have a better built failure factory. This failure factory is not the production line. Failure is a given in life and is produced by being alive. This is a processing factory and everyone has one. Failure goes in, how we choose to respond or react to it is the processing part inside the factory and our leadership effectiveness is strongly impacted by what comes out the other end, which is how we are fundamentally changed, for better or worse, by the failure.

Leaders in Gear have a positive influence on the relationships and projects in their life. This means they are able to remain positive, influence others, and grow even when failure is fed in. Having this type of failure factory requires you to:

1. Recognize and be okay with the fact that you are flawed. You need to be very honest with both your strengths and your weaknesses. See your failures as failed behavior, not as systemic failure. There is nothing more debilitating than lost hope. Remember also that no one expects you to be perfect. Just because you are a leader, doesn't mean you are without fault. People are inspired by leaders who are broken, but find a way to do great things. It makes it seem like they could do the same.

2. View failure as temporary. Set your sights on the long-term. Until the day you die, you have a chance to make things right, better and different. I have another friend named Tiffany who was diagnosed with APD (Auditory Processing

Disorder) as a young child. The doctors told her parents she would never be able to speak legibly her entire life. They took this diagnosis and threw it out the window. Tiffany and her parents worked tirelessly year after year. Through this experience Tiffany's sharpened work ethic allowed her to start her own non-profit while in high school and go to college on thousands of dollars of scholarships. When you fail or when life throws challenges your way, fight your way through them. There is light on the other side if you choose to uncover it.

3. Look for meaning and context. Actively seek out learning lessons by asking why did this happen, not just how did this happen. When you get bogged down in trying to discover the cause of a failure, you miss a golden opportunity to see the true purpose for it. Chances are good one door shut so that another one could be opened. My friend Curtis knows his accident happened for many reasons. Finally believing in God and becoming a Christian is the biggest one. He has been saved and baptized since his accident.

4. Laugh at yourself. Take the title on your business card serious, but not the person carrying it. This takes courage and perspective. Most people don't do it because they ride an emotional roller coaster. When things are good, their mood is good. When things go bad, their mood follows suite. This blocks their ability to find the positive, constructive and even humorous components of a mistake. Turn your roller coaster into a car with you behind the wheel by choosing to respond positively in the face of failure. Be pragmatic if it fits your style better. Just come right out and admit your failure, spend a few minutes recognizing it, smile a little and then get on to the important task at hand – learning from it and not repeating it.

Achieving Great Goals

14

Big MO

Epic goals get done by forgetting how to give up.

January is the official fitness crazy month. The combination of acute fudge and eggnog poisoning during the holidays and the tradition of renewal and self-promise that manifests itself as new year's resolutions get millions back into the gym and out of the ice cream aisle.

The stores are filled with workout clothes. The TV commercials have a disproportionate amount of advertising for the Bowflex, the Air Climber, the Gazelle, and the Nautilus. The rotating white box in my hometown even switches from a temporary book store to a workout facility every January and then closes in May, when we fall short on our ability to stay committed to our goals.

One of the best ways you can get your leadership in gear is to maintain a course of disciplined action toward important goals. Most people think you get motivated first and then you start or continue doing something second. This can prove effective temporarily, but poor as a long-term strategy. The best strategy is to start doing something first and then you will feel like doing it second. This takes the key ingredient of being a self-starter and a self-starter over the long haul. You have to also be a self-continuer.

Many of the ingredients to successfully finding and keeping motivation can be found by setting the right type of goals. The following formula reveals some secrets to being a successful self-continuer. It starts with setting GREAT goals. Goals set using the GREAT formula have a better chance of surviving through the hard times because they have a built-in bodyguard. When hard work is added to the equation, they have a great chance of becoming a reality.

Genuine. The goal has to be something you have identified as personally important and relevant to your life today. This is a major reason why many work goals don't get accomplished – the management didn't do a good enough job of making the company or organization goal personal and relevant to each team member. Your goal also needs to be authentic to your values and beliefs. When times get tough, if you don't deeply believe in your goal, you will get lazy and give up.

Real Benefit. You not only need to write down your goals, but you also need to write down the benefit of reaching each goal. Keeping your eye on your goal is important. Keeping your eye on the outcome of reaching your goal is more important. It's all about focus. The work involved in reaching your goal might not be pleasant or motivating, but the reasons why you are doing them are. When you start losing the will to self-continue, your attention needs to be on the benefits.

Exact. This is the biggest downfall of most of your goals. They are too general, too vague, and too broad. Your goals need to be very specific. You need to be able to know exactly when you have reached them. This also allows you to benchmark your progress. When an airplane takes off, the pilots aren't just flying around until their fuel runs out. Their instruments are set on a specific state, city, airport and runway. This allows them to maximize energy and equipment and minimize time and waste on their very important trip. Aren't your goals, time and energy just as important? Being vague with your goals allows weakness to creep in. Be strong by being exact.

Accountability. The strongest motivation for achieving goals is a combination of self-motivation to start and continue and having a support team around you to hold you accountable. You need to share your goal with trustworthy people and ask them to keep you honest about your progression. Choose wisely though. Not everyone will be a clean, powerful and positive influence on you and your journey. Choose accountability partners that will challenge, encourage and support you.

Time Factors. There are three time factors to consider. Set a *timeline* to benchmark your progress. When do you commit to start, being halfway, and finished? Make sure it is *the right time* and the goal fits into your life today. Importance isn't always enough for a goal to get accomplished. It has to be important and timely. Finally, you need to *give it time*. Great goals take effort, work, dedication, self-motivation and time. All epic goals get done because someone forgot how to give up.

Make an Impact

15

Big MO

Big impact comes from small, mundane acts.

I have a friend who is as talented as anyone I know, has moved up in his industry and makes a ton of money. But for some reason, he chooses to live an immoral and unethical lifestyle. If he only followed even a few leadership rules, his quality of life and the quality of his leadership would drastically improve. He is an example of someone who is too-good-to-do-good. You know the type - too cool to follow the simple, but really important rules, too self-absorbed to care about others and too good at what they do to be humble. These folks think that because they are talented or aren't in an official leadership role that following a few basic leadership rules won't make a difference in their life or the lives of the people around them. When, in many cases, their talent and ambition actually make them perfect candidates for something called DUH leadership - Drab, Uninteresting, Heroic.

DUH leadership is a simple set of behaviors that are basically very boring. Most require little energy to do once or twice, but require a heroic amount of energy to do habitually. Most people who struggle with their leadership impact would look at the following list of heroic behaviors and think, "Well, DUH. Everyone knows you should do those things." But then if you asked them to do a self-inventory on how many they do on a regular basis, another DUH moment occurs. They actually don't do many of them and that is exactly why they aren't making a big leadership impact - because they aren't doing the small, mundane tasks necessary to be a heroic leader.

As you read this list, your thoughts will go to those friends you have who do the exact opposite. Just because they have chosen to be average, instead of heroic doesn't mean you have to. They want you to be too-good-to-do-good on the surface because they will have persuaded yet another friend to live the average life with them. However, under the surface, even your most cynical peers want you and need you to be heroic. They know there is a better way to live, but they haven't mustered the strength to do it. You can be the spark they need.

1. Talk optimistically about the future. Leaders in Gear make things happen that millions of others didn't think could happen.

2. Follow through on every commitment you make. If you're not going to follow through, either don't make it or modify it to a form you are able to keep.

3. Talk more about solutions than problems. Don't ignore the challenges, but also don't dwell on them. Identify and then rectify.

4. Admit quickly when you make a mistake. The collapse of Tiger Woods' reputation in 2009 is a perfect example of how not to handle broken trust. He waited 80 days before saying anything. At that point, the disappointment had compounded and solidified.

5. Give your time, money or both for the benefit of a complete stranger in need. The value of your leadership bank account is measured primarily in selfless acts.

6. Create and stick to a not-to-do list. Busy Leaders in Gear rarely are short on things to do. This is why identifying a list of actions and behaviors that you commit to not doing is just as important as following a concrete to-do list.

7. Learn something today to move you one step closer to being excellent at a task you do every day.

8. When you get mad, step away from the situation before you respond. Leaders in Gear do not have the luxury of succumbing to negative, in-the-moment emotional temptations. You have too many people watching you and mirroring your actions. There is a long trail behind every action you do and an even longer one behind the negative ones.

9. Be nice. Simple. Boring. Powerful. Especially for people who are in power and could use negative, controlling emotions if they wanted to.

A good metaphor to demonstrate the power of DUH leadership is your average American millionaire. He or she is a normal, working-class person who drives a drab car, sleeps in an uninteresting home and lives a normal life. What they did to accumulate a heroic amount of wealth was small, simple, and disciplined daily acts. They spent less than they made. They started and stuck to a long-term savings plan. They placed more value in the money itself (which, because of compound interest, is worth more with each passing day) than on the things it could buy (which, because of depreciation, is worth less with each passing day). Very DUH. Very much uncommon among the masses. Very heroic.

Great First Impressions

16

Big MO

Listen and ask open-ended questions.

In 1852 Elisha Graves Otis invented a safety device that prevented elevators from falling if the hoisting cable broke. Today Otis Elevator Company is the largest elevator company in the world. What Elisha didn't invent was a safety device to prevent conversations from falling silent in elevators and during other awkward moments. Nor did he invent a method for maximizing those short windows of time many of us have to communicate our ideas to a potential buyer, our resume to a future boss or our background to a new friend.

The elevator speech is a time to quickly communicate a message. It is used in a variety of settings to create either a positive or negative first impression. Practice the following formula for any messages you know you will be called to give during networking opportunities, business meetings or socializing (who you are, what your organization is all about, selling an idea, etc.)

Opening. First impressions are made in the first three seconds. It then takes eight seconds to either confirm or deny those first thoughts. This means your first words need to be intentional, meaningful and purposeful. They should start taking the listener right where you want them to go. Not an appetizer, but the first bites of the main course. Begin with something positive, clear and non-threatening.

Target. The words you use depends on your target. Even within the same context (ex. - sharing an idea about a project to your peers), the words you use will change depending on the person's position, their familiarity with you and the idea, and the purpose of that particular interaction. This may seem obvious, but we can get lazy and very self-focused in situations like this. Being target focused means you have your attention on them. Leaving a "you are more important than me" residue on a conversation is as important as the words you say.

Intentional. This speaks to how you engage, why you engage and where you put the focus of your conversation. Most times you will have to do the initiation because people are primarily interested in talking about themselves or not talking at all. Be bold and talk first. The biggest question we have when someone starts a conversation with us is, "What are their intentions?" Answer that question quickly. Getting intentions out in the open will either grease the wheels of the conversation or shut it down quickly. It is better to not have a conversation that the other person really doesn't want to have than to waste time for both of you. You will benefit greatly by initiating the conversation in the context of something that interests them, not you. This is easier said than done, but master conversationalist get things said quickly and spend most of the conversation listening and asking open-ended questions.

Simple. Your formula for what is in your elevator speech should be simple. Your preparation should be in bullet point format. Your words should be void of confusing terms or jargon. Communicating in a simple manner is about cutting through the noise and gaining their attention quickly. Stories, while sometimes too long for an elevator speech time frame, are great because they are concrete and visual. In the next chapter we will look at an elevator speech called a branding statement.

Loyalty to Organizations

17

Big MO

Be clear and loud with your affiliations.

Leaders in Gear are passionate and highly skilled organization ambassadors. Your organization could be personal, professional or third place in nature. Third places include hobbies, associations, volunteer efforts, etc.; anything not directly associated with your home life or work life. This passion drives much of the extraordinary work you do as a leader. When you fully and genuinely believe in something, it causes others to believe more deeply in you, even if they don't share your belief.

However, the best thing it does is inspire loyalty from your team. There are seven characteristics of a Leader in Gear who consistently motivates and inspires their team to be equally passionate and committed to the organization. As you read through this list, mark the ones you do often and the ones you need to work on. Loyalty to you as a leader and to the organization cannot be faked, but can be engineered when done correctly.

1. Leaders in Gear are thirsty for helping the organization grow. You need to view your primary role as a servant. Be a leader focused on helping others. Your organizations are only as strong as the individuals within them. Give of yourself freely and your team will be inspired to do the same.

2. Leaders in Gear own a strong allegiance to the organization. Pure allegiance is a powerful force. It drives positive leaders like soldiers, parents, and twenty-year company men and women to stay committed to the cause. Be a leader who sticks with your organization through the good, bad and the ugly. The mechanisms of allegiance include loyalty to relationships, shared experiences and common values and beliefs. These are all emotional elements. How are you making an emotional connection with your team?

3. Leaders in Gear value and foster relationships within the organization. Of all the allegiance elements, the relationships piece is the most powerful. People may join organizations because of material gains, but they voluntarily commit their time because of relationships. If you are trying to mobilize your team, don't send out blast emails or have staff meetings. Those tools are useful, but not for motivation. Move people one at a time by strengthening personal relationships. Get to know what makes them tick, why they are here, what do they need to be better, etc.?

4. Leaders in Gear gain part of their identity from the organization. This concept is all around us. It exists at an NFL football game in Pittsburgh with thousands of fans waving their Terrible Towels. It is found at three o'clock at a middle school with every mini-van plastered with stickers announcing their children's academic accomplishments or sports team affiliation. It is even present with anyone accessorized with designer labels. These people are all visually and vocally proud of their connection with their sports team, thirteen year-old or Apple MacBook. You need to ask yourself, what are the personal benefits a member of your organization would receive from being vocal and visual with their affiliation with you and have you provided them the means to do so? Are you visually and vocally announcing your affiliation? If the organization is important to you, the answer needs to be yes.

5. Leaders in gear clearly understand their role in the organization. One of the simplest ways to get someone engaged in your organization is to give them something to do. This simple concept is integrated into organizations like a workplace, but needs to be closely monitored in volunteer-based organizations. The clearer the instructions and the amount of time/money/skills they will need to do it, the better. How clearly have you defined your role in your organizations and do your daily behaviors reflect this role? Ask this same question about every person on your team.

6. Leaders in Gear know and believe in the organization's core values. If we refer back to the allegiance elements, we see that common values and beliefs are a strong driving force in getting people to go to battle with you and for you. Common values and beliefs are so foundational to the DNA of an organization that many times we forget to shout them from the rooftop. If you are going to really get the best from your team, constantly remind them of the deeper, wider and more significant reasons why your organization and their work for it is appreciated and vital.

7. Leaders in Gear speak positively about the organization, its leadership and members. This final characteristic is very similar to the servant-minded one; either someone is in the habit of talking positively or they aren't. Research states that our optimist or pessimist nature is both ingrained in our DNA and is a function of the environment of our early developmental years. A price cannot be placed on the value of the subtle and forceful work positive leaders do to bring other people into the fold. However, even the most positive soul needs something to say. It is your job to continually push the good news of your organization and ideas on how to use them.

Figuring out how to communicate your organization's value in sixty seconds or less is a great way to get your loyalty in gear. This is called your branding statement. Imagine you are quickly explaining your company or association to someone who has never heard of it. Your first task is to give them a sense of purpose, scale and location. These three elements will give them a good starting place for understanding what your organization is all about. Following are a few questions to answer to begin filling in these three buckets. After you get all of them answered, build your branding statement by filtering down your answers to only the most concrete, visual and simple ones. Everything that makes it into your branding statement needs to be very specific – avoid using generalities or metaphors.

Purpose – What is the core mission statement of your organization? What is your role in that mission? Why does your organization exist? What value does it create for its members and/or customers?

Scale – How many employees, members, customers, stores, locations, schools, etc. are affiliated with your organization? How many years has it been around? Are there any famous people, inventions, creations or projects associated with it?

Location – Where are your main headquarters, satellite
offices, chapters, etc.? Also, where can I physically or
visually see the results of your organization's work? Do you
have brick and mortar offices? Does anyone in your
organization have published work in magazines, books, blogs,
or web sites?

Your second task is to give your organization a face. After
you overview the purpose, scale and location, think like a
news reporter and briefly tell me a story about one person in
or affiliated with your organization. It is the same dynamic
that occurs with any big news story. News reporters are
charged with not only giving us the full scope of the event
(purpose, scale, location), but also finding one person to
interview who can put a human element to the event.
Including this dynamic in your branding statement will help
make it come alive, be more interesting and more personable.

The sixty-second branding statement for my company is:

*"YourNextSpeaker is a leadership training and speaking
company. We design and deliver keynotes, workshops,
conferences, curriculum, books and blogs to help students and
adults develop their leadership and public speaking skills. I
have personally spoken for seventeen years and in front of
more than one million audience members. A few of my more
well-known clients are Boeing, the Oklahoma City Thunder,
the National Weather Service and the National FFA
organization. Our headquarters are located in Oklahoma, but
I have presented leadership trainings in forty-seven states, the
District of Columbia, Canada, and the Bahamas. Tiffany
Grant is a previous client whose story really best captures the
impact of what we do. Tiffany was a member of two student*

organizations we work with often, the National DECA and National FFA organizations. She attended multiple state conferences where we presented keynotes and workshops that inspired her to engage her leadership and overcome a number of personal challenges she faced. Tiffany also sought out my help to coach her with her public speaking skills. She has since graduated from high school and is attending college on scholarships earned from her academic, extracurricular and leadership efforts."

Technology

18

Big MO

You digital footprint leaves a lasting impression.

Today's leader is the most connected leader in history. Cell phones, email and social networks keep you constantly attached to your friends, family and team members. When you get your leadership in gear, you have more people and projects demanding your time and attention. These demands can be effectively and efficiently managed with the proper use of technology. The following list overviews a few of the most common tools at your disposal and some tips to follow to leverage their power and avoid their downfalls.

Email – This ubiquitous tool's benefits and features are obvious. Email is great at connecting quickly with one or many individuals and tracking project communication, but it is poor at communicating emotion and urgency. Therefore, you should always use phone or in-person meetings to communicate sensitive, complicated, or long messages. It is also too easy to ignore or not receive an email. If you need information or action quickly from others, do not rely on an email to prompt them.

Cell phone – Because every leader in the developed world older than ten years old has one, we know you do too. This sets a general expectation of connectivity. So, if you don't return a phone call, email or text message in a timely manner, it leaves a very bad impression. If you aren't comfortable with this system, you can create your own expectations by setting auto-replies to let people know when you can and can't be reached. The other important, yet often broken cell phone rule is to never let phone calls trump face-to-face interaction. Unless it is an emergency, the person in front of you is always more important than the one calling. You should also leverage downtime or road time to randomly call team members or other people you need to stay connected with. A quick check-in can do wonders to keep the cobwebs off of established relationships or to keep simple project details from falling through the cracks.

Facebook – The most popular social networking site in the world is probably either a small or large part of your life. It is the digital playground of over 400 million people on the planet. If you do have a profile, make certain you remember that Facebook has a very long memory. All of your friends can see every picture, status update and application on your Facebook. Even people who are not your friends can view pictures that other Facebook users tag you in. Keep your profile clean, powerful and positive. Student leaders struggle with this the most because many lead two lives. They are professional leaders during the day and unprofessional people at night. Facebook and other social networks make a lasting impression with their digital footprint. Make certain yours leaves a good one. Do this by posting pictures and status updates of your organization's good work – events, meetings, big announcements, projects, etc.

Twitter – The power of Twitter all depends on who within your network is using it. If you have clients using Twitter, you can quickly push key product updates and announcements. If you have association members using it, you can relay information about events, volunteer opportunities or ideas using 140 characters or less. Use the search function to find users you should follow and keyword trends.

WHAT DID I LEARN?

Capture the key leadership lessons from this section. Be specific about application and results. Where will you apply the lessons and what are the benefits of growing in those areas?

SECTION 2

GET YOUR TEAM IN GEAR

Get Teams to Work

19

Big MO

Individuals, not teams, do things.

Leaders in Gear understand a project's success needs to be based on both the overall outcome, as well as each team member's output. When judging the success or failure of a project the final outcome often has too many moving parts that are out of our control. Thus, this metric alone can sometimes be a poor test of the true success or failure of the project.

However, each team member's output during the project is controllable. Call it what you want, energy, enthusiasm, passion, drive, or ambition, high-level output is what makes great teams outperform the competition. Here are a few of the dynamics that create high-level output.

1. Engaging a core strength. This element is entirely about placement. Are you asking your team members to do something every day they are both skilled at and enjoy doing? Training and development can obviously help, but if you want to build a high-performing team your training goals should be taking people from good to great. This only occurs when their core job function matches their natural talents, abilities and personality.

2. Trusted leader. This element is entirely about you. You need your team to want to give their best every single time. They will only do that consistently if they trust your leadership and where you are taking the organization. Protect this valuable asset like you would any other precious resource.

3. Shared mission. The team's mission and goals need to be created by the team. If that isn't possible because of your organization's structure then at least each team member needs to go through an enrollment or ownership process. They should be acclimated to how the team's goals align with their personal goals and how the team's beliefs and values gel with their own.

4. Valued output. Everyone on the team needs to be clear about why their individual output matters to the team's success. There isn't an "I" in team, but there is a "ME." Teams don't get things done. Individuals on teams get things done. Each team member needs to understand how and why their work matters within the context of the team's mission and goals. This will help fuel their motivation and team-mindedness.

5. Organized decision making. There is an established protocol for how decisions are made. This doesn't mean you have to have a meeting for every decision; that's not practical. However, when you are making decisions at a meeting, follow a system. At the minimum you can follow the basics of Robert's Rules of Order: majority rules, minority has a voice, president doesn't get to vote, discussion time and decision time are separate, etc.

If your team is not functioning at the level you know they can, cross-reference this list with the dynamics of your team and look for disparities.

Work a Room

20

Big MO

People remember how you made them feel.

There are times when you will be called to host events, attend events or otherwise be in potentially uncomfortable or new situations where you are seen as the leader of the room. In these situations, it is important to remember that you can make or break the situation for everyone. If you look bored, disengaged, stressed, etc., these body language signals are read by and mirrored by a large portion of the group. However, if you look, feel and act energized, engaged, joyful and excited, these signals are picked up and mirrored. Maximize these opportunities by following the SMILE formula.

Socialize with as many different people in the room as possible from as many different groups as possible. These groups may include age, profession, school, etc. It is important to look and be active, moving and welcoming to all. It is also vital to not show favoritism to any one person or group. Avoid the urge to hang out with people you know. This will be a way to ensure you are spending your time meeting new people and forming new relationships. Do your best to remember names. Easiest way to do this is to say their name either in your head or back to them three times within one minute of meeting them.

Model what a gracious, friendly and excited leader should look, feel and be like. Even if you don't feel like it, fake it until you find it. You are the leader in the room. Your presence is felt in a large way. Make it a good one; one that makes people feel glad they chose to give their time, attention and/or money to your event or meeting.

Interested and Interesting. As you work the room and make people feel at home, be interested in what is going on with them. Have a list of standard questions you are going to ask people. Base these questions on topics of common interest: weather, career, hobbies, family, travel, current news stories, etc. Also, be interested in terms of their needs. Is the room hot/cold? Do they have everything they need? When they do ask you questions or you have an opportunity to share, have something interesting to say. Be knowledgeable about your organization, the event, yourself, etc. The point here is not to get the attention on you, but when the attention does fall on you, be worth listening to.

Laugh. Get people ready for a great event, meeting, etc. by looking like you are in a good mood. Throw a smile on your face (you will look better) and remember to have fun. Even the most serious meetings and events need a foundation of humor, laughter and positive emotion to take the edge off of the room and the people in it. You will also find that if you laugh and enjoy yourself, your stress will turn into healthy stress and you will enjoy yourself more. This is especially true when something goes wrong, which it always will.

Energy. I have attended or spoken at thousands of meetings and events. The number one strategy I use to help influence the mood and feel of the room is to express energy in my body language: walk fast, lean forward when people talk, ask questions and respond in a positive manner to questions. A week after your event, the majority of the people at your event will have forgotten what was said or what they ate, but most of them will remember how they felt when they were around you.

Handle Drama

21

Big MO

Foster healthy relationships.

If you are like most people, you know someone who always has to have drama in their life. It is almost like their world isn't complete unless someone is after them, someone doesn't like them, or something is wrong. Studies show this is true. People with drama trauma feel their life is boring and create drama to add excitement. Leaders in Gear understand that drama trauma negatively impacts their ability to create value and growth and they work hard to maturely deal with their emotions.

Drama trauma can overtake any person who is self-focused. This ME-ism creates an emotional vacuum where the person becomes overly sensitive to everything. Their self-focus makes them over-analyze every word said and every move made by others, while assuming all of those words and actions have something to do with them.

Poor decision-making creates as much drama trauma as Me-ism. Once someone breaks trust with others, it is very difficult for them to trust anyone, including their own judgment, adding to the drama.

How do you get rid of drama trauma? Volunteer. Do purposeful acts of kindness. Take up a team-related hobby. Foster meaningful and healthy relationships. Do anything you can to spend a good majority of your time thinking of something other than yourself and your problems.

Learn how to make better choices by watching and learning from others who have learned to do so. Say I'm sorry and recover trust quickly when you do make a bad decision. No one is perfect, but plenty of people are too selfish to say I'm sorry. Leaders in Gear know how to gingerly diffuse the impact of drama trauma.

How do you effectively deal with other's drama trauma? This is determined by your relationship with the person. If you are a person of formal influence over them (coach, manager, parent, sibling, etc.), you need to engage in the difficult conversation of helping them recognize how their drama is hurting the people and situations around them. Make it about their behavior though and not about them personally. Drama trauma doesn't exist in their life because that is the way life works. Drama is a given in life. However, drama is playing a negative role in their life because of changeable behavior that magnifies and prolongs the drama. Also, before you have that conversation, make certain you have a few identified ways in which you are prepared to help them deal with and overcome their trauma.

If you are not in a formal influence position (team member, friend, etc.), your task is to not be influenced by their drama trauma. Don't play their games or feed their drama by engaging in gossip, assumptive discussions, etc. Also, don't be afraid to help them see the real situation (if you are in the know.) People with drama trauma are constantly creating situations, arguments and disagreements out of thin air. Their self-created storylines are blinding them from the reality of the situations. You need to stay grounded.

Bring the Best Out of Others

22

Big MO

Decide what an amazing job looks like.

Your team will not always willingly give you their best effort. It is your job as their leader to help them discover and use their best work, ideas, strengths and talents.

The first step is to decide whether or not your people are in the right job. Knowing this requires an intimate understanding of the person and the job responsibilities. My mother, Annette Laubach, was a high-level leader in the health care industry for many years. She worked as the director of patient care services at three different hospitals in Oklahoma before finishing her career at a hospice in Stillwater, Oklahoma. At the hospice she had a lady who was a hard worker, but consistently under-performed. Upon further investigation into her situation, mom found out she was in the wrong position. This lady was an introvert and was working in a very social position. Once mom placed her in a more solo position, she thrived. She was able to give her best because her best was asked of her. When you have people in the wrong type of position, they are asked to engage a weakness every day. Only when people are asked to engage a strength can they perform at a high level.

Secondly, invest your coaching and development time talking about the duties of the job and what it takes to succeed in it. The teams you are called to lead have a great need for clarity of expectations. People can naturally give their best when they know what their best should look like, feel like and move like. As a leader, you have to decide what an amazing job is for each individual. You then have to put language to it and get them talking about it. Get things out in the open. Keep an eye on their progress and then guide them through the gap between average and amazing.

Once you get the gap between average and amazing identified, work with your team on getting one percent closer to amazing. Start small. Start with one skill, process or task. Figure that out, perfect it and then move on to another. Before you know it, you and your team will be much closer to amazing than average. Make sure no one feels like amazing has been reached. This can be as dangerous as never reaching for it at all.

Finally, bringing the best out of others requires you to genuinely care about them. Take interest in seeing them personally and professionally succeed and then communicate this by asking questions, learning what is good with them, what is a challenge for them, etc. These interactions need to be positive in nature, even when helping them improve. Again, make it about the behavior or the job, not the person. Always coach up and look for the good. The bad will reveal itself immediately. The positive is sometimes more elusive to find. It is your job to recognize the positive and emphasize it daily.

Connect

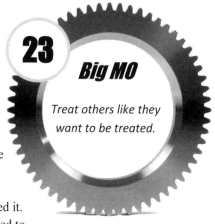

23

Big MO

Treat others like they want to be treated.

Nicolaus Copernicus (1473–1543) was the first astronomer to put the Sun at the center of the universe instead of the Earth, which was the scientific truth before Copernicus disproved it. As leaders of others, we need to take a lesson from Mr. Copernicus, take our own little world out of the center of the universe and put the true source of our power there - the people who, by choice or chance, are following us. We need to stop being so self-centered and start thinking about our people more. Some strategies:

1. Start in their world. Let your first interaction with your team be asking them questions to get them talking about their world. Immediately put your focus on them. More importantly, try your best not to judge their comments. Think of your interaction with your team in the same way a good husband interacts with his wife. Many times when she is sharing with him, she doesn't need him to make it better or add anything. What she most needs from him is to be a listening ear and a shoulder to lean on.

2. Don't make assumptions. They are based primarily on your perspective. Go straight to the information source. Drama is started and fueled by people working with and spreading bad information. Model the way for your team by seeking good data.

3. Ask for help more often. Being a Leader in Gear doesn't mean you have to know all the answers or are supposed to be right all the time. You need to be the expert many times, but your team members each play a specific role and have unique, qualified strengths. Let them shine and lift them up by asking for their opinion and advice when necessary and appropriate.

4. Adapt your leadership style to the situation. Being one-dimensional in how you deal with people is very self-centered. It leaves the impression that everyone needs to adjust to you. Connecting with your team requires you to meet them where they are or at least somewhere in the middle. Learn how each of your team members need to be led and go there. Some people require a more delicate approach and some need and want you to be more direct and bold. Some need a ton of direction and some need only to be pointed in the right direction.

> *Follow Tony Alessandra's Platinum Rule, "Do unto others as they would have done unto them."*

5. Think about the full impact range of each decision you make. A Leader in Gear's words and actions make bigger ripples on the pond than others. Keep this in mind and adjust accordingly before, during and after your team interactions.

6. Celebrate big and small accomplishments. These celebrations can be publicly or privately, depending on each person's preference. Although you are more than likely a highly self-motivated person, not everyone is gifted with such power. They need you to fuel their motivation and attitude.

Lead Without Being Bossy

24

Big MO

Use care-isma.

There are many synonyms for the word leader: captain, manager, president, CEO, officer, parent, ruler, superior, supervisor, chief, executive, guru, director, king and boss. Call it whatever you want, being a leader means you are either partially or fully in charge. How can you be the boss without being bossy?

The importance of this question cannot be understated. The number one reason why people leave their job is they don't like their immediate supervisor. Most of these situations arise because their boss might know how to get people to do things because he/she says so, but they don't know how to get people to do things because they want to. They don't know how to lead.

> *"People don't leave organizations. People leave bosses."*
> **Dr. Christy Vincent, organizational communication professor, University of Central Oklahoma**

Bossy people come in many different forms, styles and situations. I don't find myself to be a bossy person, but when it comes time to pick up the house, my young daughters see my bossy side. However, a consistently bossy leadership style breeds contempt, jealousy and anger.

If you are a naturally bossy leader (i.e. – you tend to yell at your team to get them to move), your first step is to recognize that you didn't get this way overnight and you can't improve your style overnight either. However, it is worth the effort. People should enjoy being around their leader(s). The relationship between leader and team member is one of the most important indicators of job satisfaction and you play a major role in making sure it is a positive one.

Step one is to remember that people naturally like to be around folks who are pleasant, joyful and smiling. Even the most serious job in the world demands a smile and a pleasant attitude to help everyone keep things in perspective. This doesn't mean that you run around with a cheesy smile on your face all the time. It means you try your best everyday to have a demeanor that attracts people to you. After all, trust many times begins with a smile.

Step two is to learn how to get your team to move in other methods besides telling them. There are times when the situation demands the telling approach – maybe time is limited, the task is short/small, etc. However, it is important to have other strategies in your toolbox. Here are a few options to consider with the bossiness factor highest at the top:

1. Telling Approach. Leaders in Gear are called to be the boss and there are times when you need to just tell your team to move. Moderation is the key here. Using this strategy every time will move you directly into the bossy category and you are probably missing out on opportunities to implement a softer approach.

2. Challenge Approach. People naturally like games, competitive hobbies and similar activities. The reason is because there is a challenge involved; a hurdle to overcome. Leverage these inclinations by challenging your team members, in a positive, non-demeaning way, to do something.

3. Asking Approach. Most of the time this is the approach you should use. It is proper, courteous and classic. It is also empowering because, even if they actually don't have the option to say no, many times it will feel that way to them.

4. Delegating Opinion Approach. Ask them what they think is the best move. You need a little extra time to pull this one off, but it is incredibly empowering when you allow someone else to self-direct a team decision. You can use this strategy even when you know the best course of action just to see if they create something fresh.

5. Conversation Approach. Similar to the Delegating Opinion Approach, but this approach feels more like a collective decision. Sit down with them, discuss options and decide together.

Even armed with these options, you can still come across bossy if your body language is abrasiveness. Try your best to be pleasant, welcoming, even charming. Some people call this charisma, but that word is associated with slick politicians and car salesmen. I prefer to call it care-isma. It demonstrates you care about the current situation and the nature of the influence you have on others. The purpose of charisma many times is to get the focus on you. The purpose of care-isma is to grease the wheels of the relationship by being open, interactive and demonstrating a genuine interest in others.

Apologize

25

Big MO

Deal with the relationship first.

The Hasboro® game of Jenga is a perfect metaphor for trust and leadership. Jenga is a block tower game where each player must pull out a block without making the tower fall. After each block is pulled out, it is placed back on the top of the tower. Leaders in Gear understand the power of developing the correct patterns in life that serve to maintain their tower as is. They avoid the process of taking out and replacing trust blocks by keeping their blocks in place. If and when trust is diluted or damaged, they take the time to very carefully put the block right back in place. It takes time and focus, but it is worth it.

Get into Leader Gear in this area of your leadership with others by following the Stop, Drop and ROLL pattern.

Stop. When you recognize that trust has been diluted or damaged, stop what you are doing and respond to it. Time can compound misconceptions, hurt feelings and broken trust.

Drop your pride, negative emotions and any old negative patterns that you know will prevent you from getting to the ROLL. This is very difficult to do, but it can be learned and turned into a habit with enough real world practice.

Respect the other person first. When trust has been damaged, you need to focus on the person involved, not the process. Show them you recognize you were wrong. Apologize, be humble, ask their opinion on the situation and deal with the circumstances second. Deal with the relationship first.

Open the dialogue with seeking to understand the other person's position first. Then work to help them understand your position and interests second. This is a classic example of one of Stephen Covey's seven habits of highly successful people (from the book of the same name) – seek first to understand, then to be understood.

Listen Like a Leader in Gear. After the dialogue has begun, your task is to listen like a Leader in Gear; listen intently, actively, purposefully, and openly. Don't wait to talk, purposefully listen. Maintain eye contact. Lean forward. Avoid distractions. Ask questions. Paraphrase their answers. We will dig deeper into listening in the Listen Like a Leader chapter.

Build Trust

26

Big MO

Build trust across all relationship levels.

Leaders in Gear use trust to positively influence others. You can get there by following a trust scale. This trust scale doesn't speak to the importance of trust. It is always important. This scale helps you examine and conceptualize the impact of trust when it is lost. The Fujita scale is used to rate the wind speed and thus the destructive force of tornadoes. F1 equals lowest speeds, limited damage. F5 equals highest speeds, dog is in the next state. The trust scale is rated from T1 - impact of trust loss is low, to T5 – there are major problems.

TRUST SCALE

T1 ← **Low Impact**

High Impact → T5

When you lose trust with someone, the way you can rate the impact is based on your present shared interests and relationships. If I lose trust with a stranger in Portland because I didn't let them have that cab, that is a T1. However, if I lose trust with my wife or with a key client, that is a T5.

The primary reason for rating the lost trust is to know what to do next. If you cause a T1, apologize and move on. Don't make it into something bigger than it is, but don't ignore it either. If you messed up big time and created a T5, you have some serious damage control to do. A T5, like an F5 tornado, is not easily forgiven or forgotten. It can take many months, even years to rebuild the trust in the relationship. However, if the relationship is important, it is work worth doing.

There are two secrets Leaders in Gear know and leverage:

1. Trust should be constant. The trust scale rates the trust level broken, not the person's value in the situation. Avoid rating broken trust based on how important you think the person involved is. You should always be concerned with repairing broken trust. The trust scale serves as a reminder that your strategies will be different based on the location of the broken trust on the scale. Leaders in Gear maintain trust across all levels of relationships.

2. Trust has a cumulative effect. A year's worth of T1s can have a very destructive force. I would rather work with someone who creates one T5 in our relationship, learns from it and regains my trust than someone who continually throws T1s my way. I judge how much I can trust someone based on what they do habitually, not on what they do one or two times. This is why it is important to maintain trust in the little things, as well as the big things. I have friends who have a habit of always cancelling or not showing up to events they committed to attending. As isolated cases, the broken trust rates low. Over and over again the T1s feel like T5s and it makes it hard for me to trust them in other areas.

Listen Like a Leader

27

Big MO

Fully listening is rare.

We covered the basics of active listening in the Apologize chapter, but let's quickly review:

1. Maintain eye contact
2. Lean forward
3. Mirror body language
4. Use responsive body language
5. Don't interrupt
6. Paraphrase comments
7. Ask follow-up questions

However, if you want to really listen like a Leader in Gear, you need to implement more than just this list. Let's look at listening not from a "how do I get the information better" stand point, but rather take a look at how you can get better at processing the information you do get.

It begins by looking at your opportunities to listen to your team as opportunities to provide value, change things for the better, serve them, make the most of every interaction, show you realize you don't know everything and demonstrate you are available to them. Adopting these behavior patterns will allow you to listen like a Leader in Gear and process information more effectively.

1. Provide value. As you listen, look for ways to provide value to the other person. You don't always need to provide feedback or try to improve upon what they are saying (this could hurt the conversation more than help it), but by adopting this mindset you are putting your attention fully in their world.

2. Change things for the better. There are times when your expertise is necessary and the situation is ripe for that expertise to be given. Take the initiative to listen intently, find the gaps your expert opinion can fill and fill them. If you are offering critical advice to their situation, they have no doubt you are listening.

3. Serve others. Stop what you are doing. Provide full attention to the other person. Ask questions to get them talking about things they are concerned with. All of these tactics leave the impression you are interested in them more than yourself. One person listening fully to another is the essence of being in Leader Gear. You are giving everything about you to that person at that moment in time.

4. Make the most of every interaction. Start your conversations like you were already in the middle of it. Let your guard down and be you from the very start. It is amazing how quickly people will open up to you; which is why most people don't do this. They don't want others to open up. They are not interested in listening like a leader. They would rather move on with their life. This is the perfect opportunity to demonstrate your ability and interest in being totally present.

5. Show you realize you don't know everything. This is the simplest pattern to recognize and sometimes the hardest to adopt. People who think they know everything are passively and actively encouraging others to not talk. They send signals that turn people away from them, intellectually and physically.

This isn't listening like a Leader in Gear. When you get comfortable with knowing you don't know everything, you get comfortable with saying you don't understand something. This gives someone else the chance to share their expertise. You end up listening more and this gives someone else the chance to talk more. All of this allows you to be more natural, imperfect and authentic. These are very admirable leadership traits.

6. Be available to others. This last point taps into the Leader in Gear's desire to mentor others. Being available to others doesn't mean you have to set up formal mentoring relationships. It does mean in order to listen like a leader, you have to seek out, encourage and fully commit to situations where you are providing value to someone else by being a listening ear. Say yes when someone asks to bounce an idea off you or when a younger and/or less experienced peer asks for a little of your time. Be available to share what you can.

Motivate

28

Big MO

People need to be inspired to give their best.

Motivating someone to move is at the core of the Leader in Gear's job description. Dealing with team members who are habitually unmotivated makes this job very difficult. Everyone needs to be led in their own unique way, but there are a few common ground rules you can follow to get better at motivating the seemingly unmotivated.

Identify what you mean by unmotivated for each individual. What exact actions are they not displaying that you wish they were? Be specific, concrete and visual here. Get very clear in your mind what behaviors you need them to take action on. You can't communicate instructions you don't clearly see. Asking yourself these questions will make it easier to get clear:

1. Do they know they are supposed to do those actions?
2. Do they know how to perform the actions in the manner you expect?
3. When was the last time they were reminded of those actions?
4. Are there clear reasons why those actions are important, necessary, valuable, etc.?
5. Are there clear guidelines on what will happen if they don't do those actions?
6. Are there regular or irregular sessions between you and the

person to discuss their movement from where they are currently to where you wamt them to be?

Your strategy for dealing with the unmotivated will come directly from your answers to those questions. They either aren't clear on what is expected of them, there isn't a clear reason for doing the actions, there aren't clear repercussions for not doing the actions and/or no one is coaching them to get from point A to point B.

Motive to act is always driven by self-interest, even actions by the most selfless, giving people. Your task as a motivator is to figure out which of their self-interests you can tap into.

Self-Interests

Respect from others, contribution to team, achievement of goals, self-image, job security, friendships, money, social status, avoiding pain, gaining pleasure, love, safety and personal well-being.

Your average person needs specific and clear direction in order to be motivated to act. It would nice if everyone was internally motivated to constantly scan each situation and ask "How can I help out right now in the most meaningful and purpose-filled way?" However, most people will revert to their average behavior until their better self is inspired to act. Your job is to provide this inspiration through clear, unique direction.

Find the Good in Others

29

Big MO

Begin by looking for the good.

There are three distinct types of people you are called to lead: Doers, Throughers and Spewers. Understanding which category your team members fall into will provide valuable insight into how to lead them.

Doers. These are the Type A personalities that range from the glory-seekers to the servant leaders. They are interested in getting things done. Doers see a problem, opportunity, or challenge and they take action, some for personal gain and some for the betterment of the greater cause. The upsides of the Doers are fairly self-explanatory. They get things done. They make things better, most of the time. They fail many times, but mostly because they try many times. Many of the world's greatest and smallest solutions are a result of a Doer taking action.

The downsides of having a Doer on the team are a little more complicated to explain and sometimes complex to understand. These downsides result from a Doer taking action when they don't have all the information necessary to make a decision, made a decision when it wasn't their place to do so, their decision caused them to sacrifice something more important or it wasn't the right time to take action.

Doers need only to be pointed in the right direction, celebrated for their efforts and given a good amount of autonomy. They like to feel like they play a role and have value on the team. They also enjoy a challenge. The quickest way to lose a Doer is to task them with easy or repetitive projects. They have an internal drive to create value and to grow. As their leader you need to keep this drive fueled and running smooth. You also need to take measures not to overwork them. Doers don't always have the ability to recognize when they need to take a break. They are like a sled dog. They will literally run themselves out of fuel because they love to run.

Throughers. The Througher is someone who passes through situations, events, opportunities, challenges and relationships in their life without exerting any extra effort to improve or add value. The main pro of the Througher is they don't rock the boat. Most times they don't disrupt any preexisting leadership or decision-making structures.

The main con of the Througher is they don't rock the boat. Sometimes the boat needs to be rocked. Sometimes all a problem or challenge needs is a Througher to stop and do something about it. My good friend and speaking peer Kelly Barnes says that the problem in schools today isn't drugs, alcohol, bullying or pre-marital sex. The biggest problem is good, solid students who, for whatever reason, aren't engaging their positive leadership. This clearly describes the Througher. They are just coasting through without fully getting their leadership in gear.

Most Throughers are in this category because of fear, they think their opinion, information or help isn't valuable, they are comfortable where they are and they know that many times if you talk about a problem or offer a solution, you will more than likely be asked to do something about it, they don't know how to help or they don't want to find out how to help. If you figure out the true motivation behind the Throughers in your organization, you can begin helping them rock the boat.

Spewers. The Spewer is the worst of the three. The Spewer is defined by their negative attitude and their unfortunate tendency to spew this poor attitude on everyone around them. They love to gossip and chat about how bad things are.

There are quite a few negatives of a Spewer. They don't take any positive or constructive action. They actually block the creation of positive solutions by killing the motivation, spirit, and ideas of Doers and Throughers. They have a tendency to make things worse by delaying or damaging the constructive action of others. A Spewer will highlight the negative and make the problem or challenge larger than it actually is.

These negatives make it very challenging to find the upsides of a Spewer, but there are a few. Spewers bring attention to problems, can actually provide motivation to a Doer by making them mad or annoyed, validate the importance of the Doers and show Throughers a way to get involved.

If you have a Spewer in your organization you need to sit down with them and help them recognize their behavior. Many times they have blinders on and have chosen to ignore the symptoms of their condition. Refer to the Negative People chapter for ideas on where to go from there.

Coach

30

Big MO

Ask questions to strengthen trust.

One of the most rewarding and sometimes challenging elements of leading others is helping them grow and develop their skills. My favorite leadership coach I had as a young leader (and still have as a good friend and mentor today) is the Executive Secretary of the Oklahoma FFA, Kent Boggs. Since the mid-80s, Mr. Boggs has led and guided the State FFA Officers, a team of eight college students, through a myriad of speaking events, public appearances and service to the Oklahoma FFA. His legacy will be felt for years to come because of his commitment to each team's development and growth. Early in the year and after each event, Mr. Boggs works tirelessly to coach each officer on improvement areas. His coaching sessions are intense (I served two years as an officer), not always fun, but always thorough and valuable.

This type of process requires constant attention and fostering. If you engage in employee evaluations, you are aware of how difficult it can be to make these sessions positive and productive. One way to get there is to turn your meetings into conversations and use the following five questions as the foundation. You will have other metrics and progress goals you will need to cover, but valuable, necessary and possibly surprising information can be found in their answers to these questions.

1. What is challenging you the most? Let them identify areas of improvement. Ask for specifics. When they share something you can adjust, do so. Keep in mind they are in a very vulnerable and exposed position. No one likes to have their performance judged, but it is necessary for growth. Keep the focus on their actions and how they need to be tweaked. Give them specifics on how to do that to meet your expectations.

2. What have been your best moments since we last spoke? Let them celebrate success. This is especially important during an evaluation session because you can use this time to lift their spirits and make sure they know you are seeing their contributions.

3. If you could change one thing around here, what would it be? Let them offer you advice. This can be tricky because you don't want to leave the impression something will change just because they think it's a good idea. However, your team is in the trenches every day and sees things from a different perspective than you. Leverage this perspective to get better information and make better decisions.

4. What do you need to do your job better? Once they have identified some system wide changes they would make, get more specific by asking them what needs to change just in their corner of the world. Even if nothing tangible comes out of it, just the fact that you asked and are making yourself and the organization's resources available to help them will strengthen their trust in you and your leadership.

5. What are a few great things you've seen from your team members? Let them build up their peers. This will also serve as a subtle way for them to self-identify areas where they can improve.

This approach is powerful because most evaluation sessions are one-sided with the boss doing all the talking. The conversation approach interrupts this pattern and turns the evaluation meeting into a discussion of performance and puts the focus more on the relationship instead of just on the result.

Persuade

31

Big MO

A big challenge must have a big purpose.

Leaders in Gear are called to ask others to give more, do more and be more; to rise to the challenge. Your team's performance is directly influenced by your ability to develop, frame and sell the purpose behind the challenge. Why should they give their all for the team? What are the underlying ideas driving everyone's actions? These questions must be answered and answered in very specific ways.

1. Make it personal to them. The purpose must either be entirely or partially for their benefit. If you are struggling with this one, use their language, their stories and their outcome. Frame the outcome of the challenge in terms of their rewards, benefits, etc.

2. Make it simple. Some of the biggest decisions we make in life are based on the simplest of truths. Simplicity is especially important if you are communicating to a large group. It is very difficult to effectively relay complicated information to more than a few people at a time.

3. Make it urgent. Your team is going to be more equipped to give a ton of energy today if it helps them serve a need, solve a problem or accomplish a goal they have today, not miles down the road.

4. Be Authentic. This point speaks to both your content and delivery. Just because a challenge is big and important doesn't mean the delivery mechanism has to be flashy. Conversely, authentic doesn't mean unscripted or unpracticed. Important messages demand your time, but remember to communicate the range of raw emotions everyone will experience while struggling to rise to the challenge.

A very specific area where you might be struggling with your persuasion is fundraising. Understanding how to effectively ask for money can lead to a better understanding of how to persuade people to give other items of value – time, attention, resources, etc. Let's say you agree to give twenty-five cents to a friend so they can buy a soda. What can the dynamics of that simple transaction teach us about effective fundraising?

1. He asked. Seems simple, but how much money has your organization lost simply because you haven't asked for it? How many other things have you wanted from someone that you don't have today because you haven't mustered the courage or taken the time to personally ask.

2. He asked for exactly twenty-five cents. You don't want to limit what people could possibly give, but it helped your transaction tremendously when he said he only needed a quarter. An unclear amount expectation can be a big wall. This also translates to other areas of persuasion. For example, if you are trying to persuade people to volunteer for an event, don't just ask for volunteers. Make a list of tasks and have people sign up for specific duties. I am more likely to be persuaded to help out if I know ahead of time what I will be asked to do.

3. He is a friend. Your relationship with your buddy applied the grease that made the transaction run quicker, smoother and with very little friction. My friend and fellow speaker Phil Boyte has shared the following phrase in schools across America for years, "It's hard to hate someone when you know their story." For this discussion we can say, "It is difficult to say no to someone when they are a friend."

4. He had a very specific need. You knew exactly where your money would go. He was going to buy a Coke with it. You need to be concrete, visual and simple with why you or your organization need someone's money, time, attention or resources.

5. You could relate with his need. Your friend was thirsty - a place you have been many times. This personal connection made it easier for you to empathize with him and made it more likely for you to give. You need to find a way to let your potential givers empathize with your cause. What are your shared life or work experiences?

6. You had the quarter on you and could hand it to him. This is about logistics. Dealing with what your potential givers can give is important, but just as important is where, how and when.

7. You trusted he would use the $.25 to actually buy a Coke. Why should your target market trust you? How have you built this trust? How will you continue to foster trust?

Negative People

32

Big MO

Negative people need evidence to change.

You probably have one or more negative people in your life today, either at home or work or both. These are the people that always have something going wrong, always tell you why something can't or won't happen and love to point out everyone's faults.

What is the best way to deal with these individuals? Can they have their mind changed? Why, out of all the emotions in the human spirit, have they chosen to allow a negative attitude define them? Here are three concepts to help you deal with them and make life bearable for you both.

1. They weren't born negative. They became conditioned over time. They learned this mode of operation slowly over the years. If you view their negative attitude as a pervasive condition of their life, many times this makes it easier to deal with them because you know they don't have a beef with you, they have a beef with everyone and everything. This will help you to not take their comments too personally.

2. They can't be totally positive overnight. It will take time if it happens at all. Your negative friends, family and co-workers have perfected the art of negativity. Depending on their age, they may have been negative for a long time. Don't expect overnight results or changes, but do expect them to respond, even in small, subtle ways, to your positive influence.

Your positive expectations of their behavior can make a difference.

3. You can't change them. Only they can choose to make the change. Negative people are the way they are for a reason. There is something about their personality that gets fed by being negative. They get attention. Negative people tend to bond together so there might be an element of community. It is a safe place to play. Never getting your hopes up and always having low expectations means you aren't let down as often. It is also an easy place to play because they are all about problems and not solutions. The problems are easily recognizable and take zero work. Solutions are many times difficult to see and require action to come to life. All of these reasons lead to the fact that a negative person will only change if they are presented with enough evidence that it is worth the change. This is where you can play a role. Your positive behavior and language can be this evidence. In a compassionate way, help them understand that little people talk about problems and big people talk about solutions. It's better to be big.

Controlling Leaders

33

Big MO

Controlling leaders lead from fear.

How do you deal with a leader who makes decisions and policies that have a negative impact, but they continue to make them anyway because they have an inflated need for control?

1. Be empathetic. Most of their decisions have good and valid reasons. Many times those in leadership know more about the reasons than they are either willing or able to share. However, this isn't an excuse for acting powerless. Make sure to at least ask for the reason(s) behind the decision. You can also request empathy from them. Next time they make a decision that hinders your ability to do good work, ask them (in a calm, cool and positive tone) for suggestions on how they would operate if they were in your position. You can also ask them for advice. This gesture will feed their need for power, but also force them to really think about the practical impact of their decision.

2. Ask for changes. Powerful people are just as annoyed by people who challenge their opinions and decisions as you are. However, powerful people also respect those who demonstrate power and have little respect for the weak. Your controlling leader won't enjoy you asking for changes, but they might respect you for it if you do it the right way.

3. Embrace risk. There is always a risk when you challenge the system, when you don't just lie down and when you try to take the lead. That is why it is very important to weigh the consequences and make sure it is worth the risk to fight. Sometimes it is. Sometimes it is not. Make a pros and cons list and quantify the risk as much as you can.

4. Start small. If you have a controlling leader, you probably have a list of things you would change if you were in charge. Write down this specific list and prioritize them in order of size of difficulty for them to change. Begin requesting changes, but start with the small things. If you win a few small ones, this might give you some "change capital" to use for the larger items; especially if those small changes dramatically improve you and your team's performance. Even if you don't get the larger ones changed, you at least made a few changes happen.

5. Start big. You can also try the reverse strategy. Ask for something big to be changed. Always have a plan B request that is a touch smaller than your first one. You can revert to it if they reject the larger one.

6. State the benefits. When you do ask for changes, back up the request with clear explanations of how the current way is hurting the organization and a few valid reasons for your requested change. Try your best to leave individuals out of it. Speak in terms of the potential upside for the organization.

7. Be an ally. Although difficult to put into practice, they are more likely to relinquish control if they learn to trust you more. Trust is a by-product of three things: reputation (I don't know you, but someone I trust does), repetition (you have repeatedly exhibited behavior that makes me trust you) and relationship (I know you and I like you, so I trust you). Many times in a formal organizational structure, it is difficult to earn all three, but that is your goal. The most powerful one of the three is relationship. Find ways to foster a relationship with your leader.

8. Choose positive responses. Never respond to your leader with sarcasm, cynicism, anger, jealousy or greed. Times of conflict require you to be calm, professional and positive. Therefore, don't engage with them when you are filled with a negative emotion. Take a day or two to think about it and chat with them when you have a calm head.

9. Face to face. Even though you need to remain positive, these interactions are certainly not going to all be positive. There will be difficult conversations. One of the reasons why your leader is controlling is because it works. Most people run from conflict and choose not to engage or ask for what they need because they are afraid, don't think it's their place or aren't willing to stomach the consequences. Get your leadership in gear and engage in a difficult face to face conversation.

10. It's not personal. This is not true in all cases, but many times the policies or situations your controlling leader has created is a response to their need for perfection or their need to avoid conflict. They are also many times motivated by fear of what might happen if they lose control. It is not about you so try to not take it personally. It's not that they don't trust you or want to see you fail; they just don't know any other way to lead.

Deliver Bad News

34

Big MO

The medium is as important as the message.

One of the most challenging parts of being in a leadership position is making decisions that are necessary, but unpopular. These decisions can alienate you from your team, turn friends into enemies and add friction to your relationships. How do you strike an even balance between keeping people happy (satisfied, challenged, engaged, etc.) and moving the organization forward?

> *"To be able to lead others, a man must be willing to go forward alone."*
> *Harry S. Truman, U.S. President*

One of the first things you need to decide when you step up to engage your leadership is that you are ok with not always being liked. This doesn't mean you upset people or treat others poorly intentionally. It means forward movement involves change that is often feared, battled against and unpopular. Yet as the leader, your job is to guide this change and because of your job description, you are not always going to be the most popular person.

Secondly, before you make a decision you know is going to be widely unpopular, foster a few key relationships. Have a sit down with the team members who many people trust and respect and discuss the pros and cons of your decision. Your job here is diplomacy. Do your best to communicate clearly the benefits of your move for everyone involved. You should also sit down with your most vocal opponent and listen. Make them feel like they have your ear.

We have all heard stories of people being fired by text message or divorced via messenger. These stories serve as a reminder that a message's medium is almost as important as the message itself. Zig Ziglar, the grandfather of motivational speakers, announced a major decision for his company via a company-wide email. He later apologized, not for the message, but for how it was given. It is important to deliver the message as personally as possible. This is not the easiest path, but it is the one that will earn you the most trust.

Finally, when you are in conversation with your team about their viewpoint, be as cordial, caring and empathetic as possible. The ability to gracefully agree to disagree will go a long way. However, be confident and resolute when stating your viewpoint and the reasons why you made the decision you did.

Brainstorm

35 *Big MO*

The loudest people do not always have the best ideas.

Leading group decision making is a core part of being a Leader in Gear. These meetings can be effective or ineffective based on the process used. I was called to lead a group of two-hundred educators and staff members through the process of creating a new vision statement for the school district. We used the following process and found it to be very effective at achieving the two major goals of any brainstorming session: make sure everyone has a chance to have their ideas heard and give the full group a chance to vote on the best ideas. Modify the following ideas to fit your group size and intended outcomes.

1. Small groups. Break the two-hundred into small groups of eight to ten people per group. Mix them up by job title, experience, gender, etc.

2. Targeted discussion topics. Have each group pick one of these four discussion areas: What is our greatest strength? What are our greatest challenges? What words should be included in the statement? Where could the vision statement be used? Your questions are based on the type and nature of your final product.

3. Idea capture. Give each group a sheet of flipchart paper and markers to capture ideas. Each group picks a discussion leader. This person numbers the ideas, labels each sheet by discussion area and signs their name on the bottom. They should write very legibly.

4. Key idea discussion. Each group has exactly five minutes to discuss ideas. Do not judge ideas. This first round is about quantity. Discussion leaders must not make judgments or throw out ideas. They only write. This is because they could have too much influence and power over the group discussion. They can encourage, ask for clarity or ask questions to get ideas flowing.

5. Idea swapping. After five minutes each group gets a different group's discussion sheet. The new sheet has to be on one of the other three discussion areas. Their task is to add a few new ideas to the list, but mainly to go back through the previous ideas and make them more concrete, visual and simple. This step is about idea sharpening and quality.

6. Big group voting. After that five minutes is up each group hangs up their poster of ideas. Each person then grabs three to five stickers and everyone walks around the room and puts a sticker next to an idea that they think should be in the vision statement. This is a critical step. Only vote on ideas that you think should make the cut.

7. Discuss the top ideas. Take the most popular five to ten ideas, have each team get a new easel pad sheet, write them down and discuss pros and cons. The main output goal here is for each team to whittle the ideas down to their version of a great vision statement.

8. Final voting. At this point each team gets one last poster paper and writes their final first draft of their vision statement. These are hung up. Everyone gets only one sticker this time and votes for their favorite one. You can also do this round of voting in the blind. Have each team hang up their poster. Assign each poster a number, pass out paper slips, have everyone vote for their favorite, tally up the votes and most votes wins.

9. Structure. You can do two things here. Take the winning vote as is or take the best parts of the top two or three and collectively make a final one. This really all depends on how the final ideas are structured.

This is a very thorough and quick process for taking a large number of ideas, filtering them down and creating a collaborative piece. Following are a few general brainstorming guidelines you will want to follow the next time you are leading any type of brainstorming session. These guidelines are designed to help groups make better decisions using a shorter and more effective process. They also help prevent the only ideas getting discussed coming primarily from the biggest personalities or the most experience. The best ideas do not always come from those two groups.

1. Have a pre-defined discussion leader. This does not have to be the person with the most authority in the room. It actually works better many times if it is not.

2. If you find you need more information to make decisions in the room, find it now if you can. If you can't find it now, assign someone to track it down and delay the decision making process until you have all the information you need.

3. Flip chart your ideas, number the sheets and use bullet points. Someone in the group will have to type up these notes

to refer to them later. Therefore, keep your brainstorming notes organized and clean.

4. Have a parking lot flip chart to capture ideas you might want to revisit and will distract from the current conversation.

5. The discussion leader needs to hold their tongue on their opinions. They control too much of the conversation flow energy to self-impose their will on the discussion.

6. Speak in concrete terms. Who exactly will move that forward? What exactly will that look like? Be as specific as you can.

7. Once you get a good starter set of ideas take them to a vote. You might find that everyone agrees on the same thing and you can save hours of unnecessary banter time.

8. Creating ideas is a totally separate process from making judgments on ideas. If you do both at the same time, it steals the energy away from the creation process and it inadvertently stunts the effectiveness of the judgments. Keep these two group tasks separated if you can.

Negotiate

36

Big MO

Be prepared for a no, but fight for a yes.

One common question I get often as I travel the country teaching leadership is, "How do I get things done when my boss, adviser or team leader keeps saying no and shutting me down?" Here are a few strategies to keep in mind the next time you try to create or start something new in your organization and someone is blocking your progress.

1. Understand why they are saying no. A good amount of their motivation for saying no, especially if they have years of experience, is they have been burned in the past by people who have had great ideas, but didn't follow through. Your boss may also have constraints or barriers that are only visible to them and sometimes it may be quicker and easier to use the strategy of saying no instead of doing what they should do which is to explain their position and then work to find a middle ground that will work for both of you.

2. Be prepared for a no response. Don't get so emotionally invested in an idea or project before you seek approval that a no will totally topple you. How you respond to their rejection or objections does make a difference in where the idea can go from there. Reacting with a negative emotion (anger, disgust, disappointment, etc.) is the quickest way to shut down the negotiations. Responding with a positive emotion (joy, surprise, optimism, etc.) keeps the discussions open. You can also paraphrase their response and demonstrate your understanding and respect of their opinion. However, view their "no" as a "not right now" or as a "you haven't convinced me to say yes".

3. Have a plan B. If you do get a no response, ask for an explanation why and start going to plan B with them. Plan B should be a version of plan A with compromises made. This is where the negotiation strategies begin. This will demonstrate a few things: you are committed to the idea enough to fight for it, you are willing to work with them and you have put enough thought into your idea to actually have plan B (and plans C, D, E, etc.) If your plan B doesn't meet any of their needs, go back to the drawing board and design one that does.

4. Give your plan a fighting chance. There are some strategies you can employ to give your plan a fighting chance right off the bat. Do as much information gathering beforehand as possible. Find out policies, do market research, get your team together, etc. Do some initial work to demonstrate your commitment to the project. It is important not to do too much and not to use that pre-work as a bargaining chip. I.e. don't say, "But how can you say no? Look at all the work we have already done." This is a negative negotiation strategy that will cost you trust chips with your boss. Be ready to answer questions to support and sell your idea. Most ideas get shot down early not because they are bad ideas, but because they didn't have a Leader in Gear doing a good enough job championing them.

Run Meetings

37

Big MO

Take control or the meeting will control you.

Although most meetings are unnecessary, too long and poorly managed, meetings are an inevitable part of a Leader in Gear's life. If you and your team are going to do extraordinary work, you have to have extraordinary meetings. Keep them short. Only include information that is best shared in person. Most of the data passed in face to face meetings could be shared quicker and more efficiently via email, virtual workspace, etc.

> *If you and your team are going to do extraordinary work, you have to lead extraordinary meetings.*

As the leader you need to know how to run efficient meetings. You should make it worthwhile to have everyone there. However, even if you do take steps to ensure that everyone has a purpose and is needed in the room, you will still have difficulties managing attention and keeping everyone focused. The following tactics will help you do just that.

1. Focus on the cause, not the conditions. If your meetings are full of distracted attendees, side chattering or other symptoms of disengagement, look for the root cause. A condition-focus would be, "Julie is constantly chatting during the meeting." A cause-focus would be, "Julie does not see value in the meeting and/or hasn't been enrolled in the meeting." A condition-focus will lead you to a brick wall every time and is your interpretation of the current situation. A cause-focus will lead you to seek out more information. You have to ask questions and look for the why, not the what and that will lead to a better solution of how to get them reengaged.

2. Enroll your attendees in the meeting. People will naturally give their attention to something that is interesting, unique, unexpected, engaging and/or valuable to them personally. Leverage this by doing something at the very first of the meeting to enroll them in the meeting agenda. Give everyone a question to personally answer and share with the group. Do a quick team-building exercise. Your primary goal here is to break their attention from whatever was happening before the meeting and get them focused on the here and now.

3. Remove distractions. Throw cell phones in the middle of the table. Close windows. Remove the extra space between people. Set in a circle. Get away from tables if possible. Take control of the physical environment in the room or it can take control of the meeting.

4. Set and adhere to an agenda. People are more willing to give their attention to something if they know how long that attention will have to last. Set out a game plan, set a time limit and stick to both. If something comes up off the game plan and/or will take you over time, have someone write it down and save it for a later meeting.

5. Have a recognized discussion/agenda leader. This is probably you. However, assign the task to someone else today. Chat with them beforehand about the agenda, meeting goals and time limits and then have them guide the ship.

6. Make certain you need the meeting. Many meetings go awry because they are unnecessary. It is easy to get distracted from something you don't see any value in.

7. Privately Ask, Engage, Remove. If you do all of these things and you still have a disruptive team member, privately ask them if they are aware of how their negative behavior is hurting the meeting. Ask them to help the team out by adjusting their behavior. If that doesn't work, engage them in some way during the meeting. Have them lead a discussion. Ask them to offer an opinion. If those strategies don't work, take a break and ask them to leave.

WHAT DID I LEARN?

Capture the key leadership lessons from this section. Be specific about application and results. Where will you apply the lessons and what are the benefits of growing in those areas?

SECTION 3

GET YOUR PRESENTATIONS IN GEAR

Seven Speaking Basics

38

Big MO

Give concrete, visual, simple messages.

Leaders in Gear invest a large amount of time and attention in connecting with the people they lead. Most of these connections happen informally and in a small team environment. However, presentations are also an integral part of a leader's influence tool kit. Our final section is all about how to maximize these opportunities and deliver with style, substance and success. We begin with the following seven principles that are at the core of all great presenters. We will dig deeper into each one in the following chapters.

1. Authenticity is the number one goal. The best communicators know who they are, have a real-life bond with their content and strive to make a genuine connection with their audience. The biggest challenge on the road to speaking success is getting out of your own way and letting the best of the real you shine through. Your goal isn't to be perfect, but to be perfectly yourself. This concept is so important, my speaking skills blog is titled *www.AuthenticityRules.com.*

2. Nervousness and excitement are chemically the same. To the human body, there is no difference between being very nervous and very excited. Don't worry about getting rid of your nerves. Begin down the path of controlling your nerves by thinking about them differently. Accept that it is normal to be nervous and leverage your nerves to keep you on your toes.

3. Engage your audience quickly to control their attention. Almost as important as controlling your nerves is controlling your audience's focus. Get them involved in your presentation right from the start. Ask a question. Have them share with a partner. Get them physically moving. Make them laugh. Chances are good you are more interested in your topic than they are. Your first and most important goal at the start of your presentation is to earn their attention by getting them actively involved in your presentation.

4. Send your message through the CVS test. In today's noisy world, the most effective messages cut to the core quickly. Make sure your messages are Concrete, Visual and Simple. Don't make me search too hard for the meaning. Use concrete metaphors and examples. Help me see your message by using visual cues, props, videos, etc. Finally, your audience's brains are busy places. Your message shouldn't be. Make it simple. The quickest way to achieve CVS is through good story telling.

5. Master the art of indexing and filtering. Great presenters are great at preparing their content. They index information into buckets based on a set range of categories, topics, types of content, etc. they deem necessary for their presentations. Then they fill these buckets as full as they can. The important next step is filtering down the information based on authenticity, the CVS test and the major goals of their presentation.

6. Your body language sends thousands of messages while your words only send a few. The most important body language is eye contact. You should make it with specific people and make it often. Think of any presentation as a string of smaller conversations with a number of different people. Beyond that, think moderation and variety when it comes to hand movements, walking, pace, volume, and facial expressions.

7. You can and should continue to develop your presentation skills. Communicating effectively is equal parts technical, mental and habitual. No matter your experience level, all three of these can be sharpened and improved. More importantly, because your relationships, influence level and, in many cases, earning ability are dramatically impacted by your speaking skills, you should never stop developing your ability to stand and deliver with style, substance and success.

Five Speaking Misconceptions

39

Big MO

Credibility starts with authenticity.

1. I have to get rid of my nervousness. Zig Ziglar said, "Your task is not to get rid of the butterflies, but get them to fly in formation."

Your goal is to control your nervousness, harness it and turn the negative energy into positive energy. To do this, you need to accept the fact you will be nervous, take deep breaths, confidently know your material and break down the barrier between you and the audience as quickly as possible. Also, presenters who are able to control their nerves care deeply about their audience and have total disregard for them at the same time. They care about making a connection with them, but their confidence and passion isn't shaken if the audience doesn't respond like they expect or want.

2. I have to give a ton of information to look credible. Audiences appreciate a presenter who makes things simple and who takes less time than they are given. Credibility is not accomplished by data volume, but by presenter authenticity.

> *"Any fool can make things bigger and more complex. It takes a touch of genius and a lot of courage to move in the opposite directions."*
> **Albert Einstein**

3. I have to please everyone in the audience. There are at least four different personality types in your audience at any given time. The fun-loving people want interaction and humor. The fact-loving people want data and logic. The people-loving people want stories and emotions. The order-loving people want you to know what you are doing. You can't please everyone all the time, but you can please everyone at least more than once.

4. I have to run a meeting or presentation a certain way because that is how it has always been done. This misconception is all about risk. It is shocking how many professionals hamstring their personal effectiveness and their presentation's impact because they don't understand risk always comes before value.

5. I have to assume people are not going to listen and are not going to get involved because they don't for anyone else. If you don't take control of the room, the room will take control of your presentation. The speaker to audience ratio makes the old axiom, "expectations equal behavior" hold very true for presentations. Most audiences don't actively listen to presentations because they aren't worth listening to. Yours should be different.

Three Common Pitfalls

40

Big MO

Give your talks zest, flavor and life.

You have a variety of forces working against your ability to be the best of yourself as a presenter. These forces mask your authenticity and should be viewed as enemies. You need to know them intimately and you need to fight them. Following are three of the most enduring enemies presenters battle.

1. Tepidness. You must be engaging as a presenter. If you take a tepid approach to your content, topic, audience or the actual act of presenting, you are telling your audience not to listen. This tepidness comes across primarily from your non-verbals, which make up the majority of your message's meaning.

Lukewarm Non-Verbals to Avoid

Monotone speech pattern
Lack of eye contact
No variety in facial expressions
No smiling
No variety in volume
General lack of gestures

Tepidness is also revealed by using weak language. Weak language includes words like kind of, sort of, maybe, and possibly. These words leave the impression you are saying one thing, but either don't firmly believe it or aren't passionate enough about what you are saying to take sides. Don't sacrifice passion for diplomacy.

2. Separation. Our second enemy is the most relevant to your audience because it concerns their world; not connecting with your audience. You should be very concerned about separation from your listeners. This enemy can be defeated both on location and during the preparation process.

On location you can start connecting with your audience even before you start speaking. Mingle with them, ask questions, demonstrate interest in their answers by asking follow-up questions and learn names. During your presentation, make direct eye contact, avoid using a podium, use the names you learned and be aware of any sensory needs they might have; lights, temperature, microphone volume, outside noise level, etc.

You can also help ensure a strong connection with your audience by doing your homework far in advance. Ask yourself questions about your audience and then build both your content and your technique around the answers.

3. Blandness. Your job as a presenter is to move your audience in one or many of the following ways: intellectually (to teach), emotionally (to inspire), physically (to direct) and/or conceptually (to show). Movement requires attention. Attention requires motive. Your audience will listen to you, believe you and even act upon this belief if you give them a good enough reason. One of the best reasons to listen is newness, freshness, creative ideas, etc. If your presentation is bland, your audience will start checking out. The blandness enemy shows up most commonly in two areas; logistics and content.

Logistics Blandness. When a presenter does things the way they have always been done: same room set-up, same visual aids, same presentation length, same audience interaction, etc.

Content Blandness. When a presenter uses content that is safe, but over-used: commonly used quotes, stories, facts, data, etc.

Your audience members' brains require fresh stimuli to motivate attention. Give it to them. Give your presentation some life, zest, excitement, and flavor. They will not only thank you for it, but they will also be more willing and able to take action. This is the hallmark of all truly authentic presenters. The experience and their content have a long life because it is unique and thus easier to remember.

This list of enemies is in no way complete. However, if you tackle only these three enemies, you are well on your way to creating a room full of friends.

Create Memorable Messages

41

Big MO

Less information is more.

You enter a room labeled Numbers Room. You see fifty people walking around with name tags on and they look like this: 3947202734, 2739475214, 0481659123, 3927511198, and 2847111873.

You then leave and enter a different room labeled Names Room. You see fifty different people walking around with name tags. Only this time the name tags look like this: Bob, Steve, Julie, Rick and Tom.

Which room would you expect to remember more people's names? The answer, of course, is the Names Room. Remember this the next time you need to deliver a message that you want to stick. The people in the Numbers Room might very well be thoroughly and accurately labeled, but the chances their names would be remembered are slim to none. To deliver a rememorable message, leverage the secrets of the Names Room.

1. **Short.** Less information is more.

2. **Easily Recognizable.** Short names and unique faces work for humans. It helps us to recognize people we know. Use this principle to your advantage by avoiding the use of jargon, unfamiliar metaphors and data that doesn't directly support your points or strengthen your message.

3. Easily Recallable. Close your eyes and repeat the word Bob. Now close your eyes and repeat the number 3947202734. Big difference. Use simple words and phrases to "stickify" your message.

5. Overcomes the Knowledge Gap. You probably have never seen 3947202734 before.   Your mind has to work harder to try to remember brand new information. However, you have heard, seen and dealt with the name Bob all your life. Find a way to take pre-existing words, concepts, or labels and give them new meaning.

Control Nerves

42

Big MO

Know your stuff top to bottom.

When it comes to public speaking, nerves are like audience members; always there, a necessary part of the process and not always pleasant. However, like audience members, nerves can either help you or hurt you depending on how you think about them. Follow these rules to turn controlling nerves into a piece of CAKE.

Change your perspective. You can quickly convert your nervousness into excitement by changing the way you think about what is going on. This is a great example of "change your mind and the rest will follow." Also, nerves are a necessary part of the process. It is your body's way of telling you this is important, critical, interesting, different than normal, etc. Therefore, to harness the power of this natural response, change your goal from getting rid of your nerves to controlling your nerves.

Audience-focused. Get your mind off of you and your content and put your focus on your audience. Talk to them, be in their space, ask questions, sit in the room like one of them, etc. It helps to remember your audience wants you to do good. No one likes to sit through poor presentations. They want you to be worth listening to. I know at times it doesn't always feel like it, but they are on your side. Your job is to get on their side.

Knowledge. Knowing your stuff top to bottom is the number one way to control your nerves. If you need to memorize your content to reach this level of control, then do so. Some say that memorizing content makes you look like a robot. That is not true. Robotic delivery of memorized content is the enemy here. Does your favorite actor/actress look like a robot on the screen? No. Are their lines memorized? Yes. Many of the best presenters memorize a large portion of their content. The presentation doesn't feel memorized because they invested a large portion of time on their delivery skills.

Experience. The more you do a task the better your body and brain get at responding to the emotions and physical elements related to it. Speaking in public is very much a physical, mental and emotional art form. Getting up and speaking a ton is the best medicine for a bad case of the nerves. Of course, you need to be practicing and doing the right things. There are literally millions of golfers who have been golfing for years, but still are horrible golfers because their experience only allowed them to perfect their bad habits. To get good experience you have to get good coaching. Seek out someone who knows what to look for, have them watch you, coach you and then work on their suggestions. The key here is to find someone who has an expert eye. Everyone has an opinion on what they like or dislike about speakers. Only an expert presentation coach knows how to look for what you need to specifically do to get better.

SMART Presenters

43

Big MO

Broken time rules kill presentations.

Smile. This speaks to the fact that your interaction with the audience should be one of "how can I serve you?" View your audience as customers you aim to please, not people you need to control. Don't sacrifice authority and orderliness for this, but this should be your base camp to work from. This also speaks to the truth that your audience will enjoy the process more when you are enjoying the process. Have fun and be in the moment.

Movement. People need to be engaged through movement; physically, mentally and emotionally. Engage them in all three ways by incorporating experiential activities in your presentations. These can range from games to demonstrations to role playing. Make sure you don't fall in the trap of choosing an activity before you choose your points. Always figure out what it is you want to say or teach first. Also, remember that we don't learn by doing things. We learn by talking about the things we do. This means your debrief is critical. Begin each activity's debrief by asking a version of what my speaking peer Bill Cordes asks, "What was this activity designed to teach us?" This gets them thinking critically and connecting the dots on their own. You should also have a short list of other questions, some rhetorical in nature, that will help your audience begin making the connection between the activity and the lesson you are teaching. Reference the Keeping Attention chapter for more tips on making the most of these audience interaction moments. If you need some new leadership activities and exercises, check out my *www.PersonalLeadershipInsight.org* website. You can read more about those leadership teaching/training resources in the PLI Curriculum section of the Appendix.

Attention. Much of group facilitation is attention management. You can encourage attention with your group by being on high-receive yourself, handling disruptions appropriately and in a courteous manner, encourage discussion through asking questions, prompting the audience members to build off of each other's comments and encouraging them to take notes. Attention management can also be improved by setting room expectations. Make sure you post these in the room and help the group stick to them. The following list contains five expectations you should be setting with your audiences:

- Be Alert
- Be Social
- Be Involved
- Be Clean
- Be Nice

Rememberable. You want to help your audience have a rememberable time; something they will want to remember and memories or content they will want and need to revisit often. You can fuel this memory creation by encouraging them to risk boldly, engage fully in group activities, and stay in the meeting room as much as possible. You will also want to use as many visuals in the room as possible. If you have a smaller group (5 – 100), use flipcharts to capture thoughts, reinforce your points, etc. For larger groups, utilize slide shows. Refer to the Powerful Slide Shows chapter for more information on how to do these correctly.

Time. A successful event, meeting, or conference experience has many moving parts. The biggest moving part is time. Here are a few time rules you should follow.

3-Second Rule. People develop a first impression of you in the first three seconds. Many times this is before you even meet them. Be mindful of how you look the moment the audience sees you. Maximize this time by appearing calm, collected and in control. A pleasant demeanor (smiling, eye contact, saying hello, etc.) helps the audience begin to trust you.

30-Second Rule. Listeners either check-in or check-out in the first thirty seconds. Get them engaged quickly – physically, emotionally, socially or intellectually.

5-Minute Rule. People constantly look for meaning and purpose. They need to either find personal meaning in what they are hearing and/or be told something that they can use every five minutes or so. Give them tangible, real ways they can take action on what they are learning or experiencing.

7-Minute Rule. Listeners need a change in how they receive information every seven minutes. This could be listening to the speaker, reflective thought, table discussion, partner discussion, taking notes, seeing something happen, or engaged in an activity that combines many of these. Most boring presenters have low energy, no variety in their body language and totally disregard the seven-minute rule.

90-Minute Rule. When meeting in big groups, listeners need to unplug from the meeting every ninety minutes.

These time rules serve as benchmarks you can use as you are building your presentation's flow. However, giving presentations can be a messy and unpredictable experience. Things are not always going to go as planned. You need to have a few back-pocket options you can employ if you are left with extra time at the end. These could include an activity, a self-running slide show, a group discussion, etc. Never end your presentation by asking for random questions. You want your ending to be powerful and tight. Nothing kills a great ending faster or more completely than asking for questions and hearing crickets. If you want to have a Q&A period, hand out index cards or note paper at the first of your presentation and ask everyone to write down questions they have as you are going through your talk. Start collecting these during your presentation (on break or while the group is active doing something) and this will help you gauge if there are any questions and how long it might take you to get through them at the end.

The more common time challenge is running out of it. If you start late, aren't given as much time as you were told or are mid-presentation and can tell you won't have enough time to finish all your material, make adjustments and do not go over time. Do not go over time. Do not go over time. Do not go over time. Do not go over time. Do not go over time. Did I mention that you should never go over time? When a speaker goes over time, someone is getting upset, annoyed or frustrated over it. Your final points are never as important as their frustration. Take something out. Prioritize your material beforehand and be clear on what absolutely needs to be said and what can be taken out. Going over time is not just about scheduling or sticking to an agenda. When a speaker goes over time, it is an act of selfishness that says, "My material and I are more important than whatever else you had planned." Never find yourself in this situation.

Develop Presentations

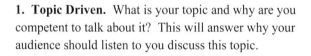

44

Big MO

Quickly figure out your unique position.

When you begin to develop a presentation, you need to quickly figure out what is unique and authentic about your take on the topic. Follow these steps as a guide to discover the foundational language for your presentation.

1. Topic Driven. What is your topic and why are you competent to talk about it? This will answer why your audience should listen to you discuss this topic.

2. Audience Driven. What are the symptoms? This is the connection between the topic and the audience members' lives. How do they know if they are affected by the problem, project, opportunity or idea you are presenting?

3. Presenter Driven. What are the solutions? What are your unique, authentic and relevant answers to their questions? Are you telling them something they have heard a million times or are you telling them something new?

4. Behavior Driven. What are the basic, relevant tasks to accomplish the solutions? Make them CVS; concrete, visual and simple. Help them see how they can start taking action today.

5. Stickiness Driven. What is your unique position statement? This is what will anchor everything you say and do in your presentation. This statement should be short, have very unique language, be action oriented, and be positively-driven, not negatively-driven. It should tell your audience what to do, not what to stop doing.

After you iron out your unique take on your topic your next task is to begin planning out your presentation. This is called your flow. How are you going to start, finish and help your audience follow your progress in the middle? Here is a simple strategy I have used thousands of times in my seventeen year speaking career.

Begin by asking, "What is at the core of my presentation?" Your answer should be the most important concept, idea, or learning lesson you want the audience to walk away with. It should be simple, clear and meaningful. Everything in your presentation should make your core stronger, simpler to understand, and easier to remember and implement.

Detail out the presentation logistics: number of people, presentation length, room set-up, audience ages, backgrounds, reasons for being there, expectations, etc., AV tools at your disposal, and organization makeup, history, challenges, etc.

Brainstorm a long list of options to support your core that fit with the logistics. Your list will include stories, more points, quotes, visuals, pictures, props, activities, exercises, videos, handout pieces, facts, data, etc. This list should be intentionally long. Everything won't make it into the presentation, but you need to get all your options in front of you.

Now you are ready to start putting together your flow. This is an exercise in pulling elements out of your options list and moving them into your outline based on these characteristics: powerful, fresh, creative, deep in meaning, easy to understand, authentic to you and connects back to your presentation's core. Take into consideration the time rules we covered in the last chapter and plan on using only eighty-percent of your allotted time.

This strategy will work for short presentations (one to ten minutes), keynotes, workshops, breakout sessions, organization meetings and informational presentations.

Small Group Credibility

45

Big MO

Smile and express genuine charisma.

Developing credibility in a small group environment is sometimes very challenging. There isn't a big stage providing you with instant expert positioning. Many times small group presentations happen in people's own company, school or organization. This can lead to them giving off the impression that they see you as the outsider. This also can lead to the group members, who probably know each other well, bonding together and either intentionally or inadvertently creating a barrier between you and the group.

The biggest tool you have to overcome this is your content preparation. Know your stuff and be ready to provide real, tangible value. You also have to establish your personal credibility, but if you have the knowledge part ready, you can do this by establishing trust in you as a person.

Trust establishment is a tricky game in this type of quick, short-term format. You don't want to leave the impression of the slick, overly-charismatic type, but you also need to break down barriers quickly. Learn names and find common ground with the group members. Ask questions about their expectations of the presentation, their job role, etc. Express genuine interest in learning about their world.

Also, make an effort to discover the big elephant in the room, if there is one. Express your concern about it and get everyone's take on it. This shows your interest in learning from them, as opposed to setting up the sessions as a one-way conversation.

Smile, be friendly, and express genuine charisma. If necessary, mirror the participants' body language to connect with them in a passive way. If they are sitting, you sit. If they are chatting, you chat. If they are discussing a news topic, you join in. There are many other small body language cues that communicate confidence. Employ as many as you can: smile, calm demeanor, direct eye contact, asking questions, well-groomed, conservative attire, standing tall, sitting tall, leaning forward, taking notes, speaking clearly, using simple, clear and firm language.

Lead Small Group Discussions

46

Big MO

Get everyone engaged to improve output.

Small group discussions, when done well, are a beauty to watch. When they are done poorly, they can damage not only the group, but the credibility of the discussion leader. My wife has been involved recently in two Bible studies for women. They had entirely different productivity levels mainly because of the skill level difference between the two facilitators. Here are some guidelines to follow the next time you are leading a small group discussion.

1. Have a casual presence. This will put you and your group at ease and grease the conversation. However, it is also important to remember that you need to bring the energy to the group. Your eyes, body language and vocal patterns need to model engagement and energy.

2. Learn names. Address each individual by name and be personable with them. It is too easy for small group discussions to have a formal, stuffy feeling and this environment prohibits open comments from the group. Keep it loose.

3. Set time limits on discussions. This is especially important if you have a set number of topics to get to that concern different members of the group. The easiest way to shut down someone from adding value to the conversation piece is to make them feel like their topic won't be discussed.

4. Mix up cliques in the room physically and conversationally. Have them sit in different parts of the room and try your best to prevent certain group members from only engaging with their friends.

5. Paraphrase comments from the group to make sure you fully understand them. This will also help the group members process any longer, jargon-filled or fragmented comments.

6. Keep things active. Make certain the group gets to physically move around at least every sixty minutes or so. This could be switching chairs, breaking into smaller groups to discuss what they've learned so far, doing an experiential activity to strengthen a certain lesson or actually taking a break. A quick boost of movement is the same as a quick boost of attention energy and leads to a more tuned-in and valuable group.

7. Encourage note taking. This can serve as a passive way to keep everyone connected to the conversation. You should model this for them. Don't forget to have someone capture relevant, revisit-worthy information on a flip chart or laptop for later discussion or review.

8. Monitor disruptions. Call out anyone who is actively being disruptive or harmful to the group process. Best case scenario is to do this in private and away from the group. You won't always have the time or space for that. So, a gentle, verbal nudge in the group can be helpful to get them back on track.

9. Focus. Do your absolute best to keep the discussion focused and on track. Your primary role as the discussion leader is not to bring value to the group through input, but rather through leadership and thought direction.

Room Preparation

47

Big MO

Your presentation starts before you do.

Trainers and speakers who use icebreakers operate from a flawed theory of presenting. They think they need to use the first few minutes of their time building rapport and getting their audience warmed up to each other, the content and the presenter. A better theory is based on the fact that you have about thirty seconds to get buy in from an audience member. This means the warming up needs to happen even before you officially begin to maximize the power and effectiveness of those first, critical thirty seconds. Therefore, you should get the audience engaged in the experience of the presentation before you start talking.

This audience engagement should be driven by an active, colorful and inviting room atmosphere.

The Walls - Filled with messages. Pre-designed flipcharts with key words and phrases. Possibly a self-running slide show on a big screen introducing the audience to the content.

The Air - Filled with music. Pick tunes that put the audience into the mood you want them to be in – happy, solemn, upbeat, dancing, etc. The air should also be a touch cooler than normal. Your energy and their involvement will warm the air after you get started. You can access the upbeat and/or reflective playlists I use in my programs by typing "iTunes" in the search box at *www.AuthenticityRules.com*.

The Speaker- Filled with energy. You should be in their space asking questions, shaking hands, making sure they have everything they need, building rapport and learning names.

The Chairs - Filled with people. Take out any extras so that every chair has a person to go with it. The easiest way to kill the interaction is to allow people to sit in the back and with gaps in between people. If they do sit in the back of the room no matter what you do, then present from the back and just have everyone turn their chairs around.

The People - Filled with purpose. Give the audience something to do the minute they walk in – an activity to be finished before you officially start, a question to be answered, people to meet, etc.

Build Audience Rapport

48

Big MO

Orchestrate their involvement.

I caught the rock band Shinedown at the San Diego House of Blues in September 2009. I knew I would be hit with a wall of sound, but I didn't expect to be overly impressed with the audience rapport skills of Shinedown's lead singer, Brent Smith. After the first ten minutes of the show, he had everyone in the room not only loving the show, but also respecting him as an entertainer, crowd leader and man.

After the opening song, he gave a heartfelt thank you to everyone for coming and paying hard earned money to be there. He graciously put the thanks on them. He even said their city was beautiful, which granted we were in San Diego, but even when you compliment something obvious to a crowd of people, they respond positively. Lesson: put the focus and thanks on the audience quickly.

After the thanks, Brent did something I have never seen at any concert, he had everyone give a high-five or hand shake to someone next to them. We do this all the time at our speaking events to break down barriers between audience members, but in this venue Brent did it for a different very obvious reason. The room was full of hard rockers and fights are common. Lesson: get the audience interacting with you and each other quickly.

Twenty seconds into the third song, he stopped the song because a fight did break out in front of the stage. He physically and vocally intervened and let everyone know that tonight was about the music and having a good time, not being stupid and fighting. He waited until the two either made up or left. The entire crowd went crazy clapping when this went down. Everyone knew what type of night it would be from then on; all about the music of hard rock and none of the rest. Lesson: control the room or the room will control you. It's not that a fight will break out at your event, conference or meeting, but losing control also looks like disengagement, side chatting, texting, no learning, no emotional buy in or a host of other behaviors.

He got the crowd involved in the singing. Most of the time they were singing anyway, but he took one song and orchestrated their involvement. The cool thing is that it was at the start of one of their new songs that not everyone was familiar with. They were after he finished. Lesson: involving the audience in a big, meaningful way increases all the things you want increased during and after your presentation: entertainment, learning, retention of content, retention of the experience's feelings, etc.

He introduced a hard rock love ballad by saying that every man there was about pride, hard work and integrity, but we would be nothing without our women. He made great points quickly and honestly and even the single dudes in the room could respect the foundation of his logic. Lesson: speak from the heart. There are very few presentations where the heart isn't appropriate to bring into the discussion. It connects with everyone.

Engage an Auditorium Audience

49

Big MO

An auditorium's cons can be pros.

Auditoriums are perfect venues for presentations for many reasons. The acoustics are almost always solid. Many auditoriums have great sound systems, although I have been in quite a few that could use an upgrade to a system that doesn't have an 8-track player. The audience can see you easily and, depending on the lighting, you can see them clearly. The audience is all facing the same direction.

The main problem that can occur with auditoriums is related to their rigid structure. The seats are right next to each other and bolted to the sloped floor. This makes group interaction difficult, but not impossible. Also, depending on the size of your audience in relation to the auditorium, people can hide very easily in the corners or away from other people. This can steal energy away from the group and your presentation.

You need to take charge of the auditorium seating arrangements and rope off the back rows. Then do whatever it takes to get the audience seated in the middle sections and towards the front. The closer you have the audience to one another, the more you can do with them and the more built-in attention you will have. The best way to do this is to not give them options. Make it a requirement to sit in certain sections and to not sit in other sections.

Regarding the rigid structure, audience movement is limited, but not totally gone. Here are a few ways I use movement in auditorium settings to get everyone physically, socially and actively engaged in the program.

Random mingling. They can still stand up and meet and greet a handful of people that are seated to their left, right, front or back.

Teams. You can still get them into teams. The best set-up here is teams of six; three people from one row and three from the row behind or in front.

Quick switch. Ask everyone to switch seats with someone. They can move as far as they want. Those who are really ready to be social will really move. Those who don't will move one seat over. Either way, you get a quick jolt of energy and movement.

Pair share. Have them discuss with a person to their left, their right or in a different row.

Big group movement. If your presentation is high-energy and fun in nature, find activities where everyone does the same thing and where that thing involves movement.

Keeping Attention

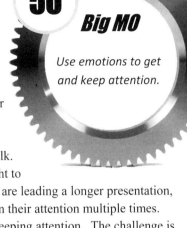

50

Big MO

Use emotions to get and keep attention.

If you earn the audience's attention, you have won a battle, but there is still a war to win. Your audience members' brains can think much faster than you can talk. This means you have to fight to keep their attention. If you are leading a longer presentation, you might even have to earn their attention multiple times. Here are six strategies on keeping attention. The challenge is listed first with the solutions second.

1. Volume. Having a microphone will normally take care of this one. However, that is not always the case. If there is a microphone, before the presentation begins practice with it a few times and find out how loud your voice needs to be so it is heard. Even with a microphone, more times than not your volume needs to be louder than normal. If you don't have a microphone, you can create triggers to focus their attention. Triggers are phrases or actions that invoke a certain response from everyone. Introduce these early in the presentation. Be sure not to overuse them; too much of a trigger will produce the same result of not having one at all. They will ignore you. Examples are: when I say "cheerio" clap three times and look this way, repeat after me, I say Batman you say Robin.

2. Round Tables. This configuration is great if your audience will do a good amount of writing, but it absolutely kills a trainer's ability to maintain order, attention and focus.

If your presentation is shorter than ninety minutes, get rid of these distractions by packing the audience in the front or back of the room with just their chairs and books. This strategy gets everyone seated close together and points all the chairs in the same direction; both help you to get and keep attention.

3. Listening Fatigue. Follow the seven minute rule. The audience needs to change the way they input information every seven minutes or so. (Read about more time rules in the SMART Presenters chapter.) The different techniques you can use are: talk to them, they talk to each other, a group member speaks, group discussion, reading something, thinking or reflecting, listening to music, watching a video, demonstrations or activities. Adhering to this time rule will create a pace to your presentation that doesn't allow for the audience to lose attention. When you are asking for group discussion or individuals to speak up, be mindful of how you ask. You never want to just ask a cold audience for comments. Fear and peer pressure will prevent 99.9% of them from speaking up. Allow them to warm up by following the SPG formula – Solo, Pair, Group. Have them write or think about a question. Have them share their answers with a partner. Then ask for answers. 90% of the time you will get more answers using SPG than without. If you don't have time for SPG, then either ask rhetorical questions (you don't expect a response, you just want them to think about it) or close-ended questions where their responses can be yes/no or one-word answers.

4. Information Overload. Especially in a long day or long session format, this concept is critical. Information overload kills attention span. The best formula is to take the very top one, two or three concepts, ideas, questions or training points and go deeper into those few. This formula trumps the "cover ten to fifteen points" formula every time because after one or two hours the audience's information receiving pipeline is full and they start shutting down. They are getting way too much information to handle and ultimately they learn less even though more content is covered.

5. Hearing the Same Old Stuff. As soon as your audience starts to hear something being covered that they have heard before, their natural response is to shut down their listening. Your task is to say the same old stuff, but to say it in new ways using your unique language, labels and viewpoint. A simple example is using quotes from famous people. These can inspire thinking and action because the celebrity or historical figure's words carry credibility and weight. However, when you start saying, "Ask not what your country can do for you…" your audience starts checking out mentally. A better strategy is to use an unknown quote from a well-known person. Check out the leadership activities and resources on my curriculum website at *www.PersonalLeadershipInsight.org* if you are looking for fresh, new activities and exercises.

6. Lack of Rapport with Presenter. A few rapport-building techniques: humor, mingling with the audience, learning their names, having high expectations of them, laughing at yourself, making your content fun, putting a competitive drive into your content. These techniques will also help you to connect with them on an emotional level. Different styles call for different emotional connections. Every style has an emotional connection that can be brought to the table, it is a matter of figuring out where that sweet spot is for you. Great presenting is about transferring emotion. By tapping into that vein with people, they almost can't help but stay attentive and focused because they are drawn to you and the emotions you are stirring in them.

Difficult Audience Members

51

Big MO

Once you lose control, you lose trust.

Uncomfortable situations with audience members can and will arise throughout your presentations. There are steps you can take to prepare yourself, your room, your content and your audience in advance to help diminish the likelihood of these situations causing real problems. It begins with having a working understanding of the different levels of instigators and knowing how to handle each. We will examine four levels in the next few pages. Hopefully it won't come to this, but if you do have to engage a disruptive audience member, be as cordial and pleasant as possible. Do not allow an unpleasant person make you or your presentation's experience turn unpleasant. You can't always prevent the storm, but you can remain calm during it.

1. Blue Level – Reconnaissance Work. As I've mentioned a few times in this section, you need to build rapport in the room; learn names, be in the audience members' space, ask questions, learn expectations, etc. If you sense or if you have been told directly there might be resistance in the room, plan accordingly. If it is only one or two people, approach them before the program and discuss options. If it is a large portion of the group, build strategies into your presentation to deal with that reality: use inclusive language, speak to the facts, stand your ground, respect other opinions, don't pass the buck, be cordial, etc.

2. Yellow Level - The Passive Dissenter. The Passive Dissenter does not mean harm. Their behavior is disruptive, but they are not intentionally trying to hurt your presentation. They are more than likely unfocused or distracted and need to be more directly engaged in the program. Catch them at break or when the big group's attention is on something else and point out how their behavior is disruptive. Ask them how they could adjust their behavior to better fit the needs of the group. Let them come up with the solution first. Give them a purposeful, if even passive, responsibility. Ask the Passive Dissenter to be a small group discussion leader, help with a small logistical item, think about some new ideas for the current discussion, etc. Get them purposefully engaged in the moment and chances are good their energy will transform from a negative into a positive.

3. Orange Level - The Aggressive Dissenter. The Aggressive Dissenter is looking to be disruptive, but not because of you. Their dissention is an outward expression of some inner strife: personal, professional, emotional, social, etc. There is a possibility they can be brought back. When you have a break, approach them one-on-one and in private. Bring the results of their behavior to their attention. Ask them if they are willing and able to set their personal agenda aside for the betterment of the group. The Aggressive Dissenter also needs a diversion to get their thinking and emotions back with the group. Let them know you are interested in them, but will not sacrifice the goals of the presentation or the interest and safety of the group just because they are having a bad day.

4. Red Level - The Aggressive Combative. The Aggressive Combative is out to get you; either because of you personally or because you happen to represent the focus of their aggression. They need to be dismissed as soon as possible. If you can, have someone else in an authoritative position do this for you and then move on. If not, then handle it yourself cordially at first, then aggressively if you must. Never get physical though. Always leave a safe zone between you and the Aggressive Combative.

The big idea driving all of these strategies is control. Once you lose control or are perceived as losing control, you lose your audience's trust. Once that is gone, everything is gone.

Four Audience Types

52

Big MO

Response always has a reason.

It is important to know in advance who you are going to have in your audience. Why are they there? What did they come to learn, do or see? Who are they? Here is a simple breakdown of how to understand an audience member's motivation walking in the room.

Passionate Paul - "I absolutely want to be in the room."
I am here to learn something specific that will help me either solve a problem or add to a solution I am currently experiencing.

How to Spot Me. I am sitting in the front rows, asking you questions beforehand, taking notes and challenging you for more, better, deeper, more specific information.

How to Connect With Me. Give me your best content up-front. Quickly let me know you have what I think you have. Win me over with substance.

Curious Chris - "I think I want to be in the room."
Your program title looks interesting, you look interesting, etc. I don't have an urgent need for your content, but I think I might like you and/or your content.

How to Spot Me. I am cordial toward you. I am basically like Passionate Paul, only I'm not quite as eager or anxious.

How to Connect With Me. Make the experience great. Attack all my senses with music, interaction, reflection, information, etc. Win me over with interestingness.

Social Sally - "I have ulterior motives for being here."
I am here because my friends are, my co-workers are, or it is the better than being somewhere else. I am not really interested in you or what you have to say.

How to Spot Me. I will be checked into the room, but not checked into you or what you have going on. I will be chatting with my people in the room and/or texting/calling my people not in the room.

How to Connect With Me. To get to me, you are going to have to go through the side door. You can't hit me directly with information or even interaction. I will put up a wall. Ask non-responsive questions that I may have wrestled with recently. Tell a story that I can relate to. If you do interaction, let me stay with my friends. Win me over with indirection.

Hostage Harriet - "I absolutely don't want to be here."
I am here because I was forced to be here. I didn't have a choice. If I had a choice, I would certainly choose to be somewhere else.

How to Spot Me. Arms crossed. No eye contact. No response to questions. I might be abrasive or disruptive, but not necessarily.

How to Connect With Me. Don't force the issue. Assume I'm not in the room. If I try to disrupt you, deal with me quickly and privately. Be real with me, though. I'm still a person with emotions. My barriers are up higher than others, but you can't take them down. You have to give me a good reason to take them down on my own. Win me over with respect.

Great Keynotes

53

Big MO

Be fully engaged.

My day job is traveling the country delivering everything from short keynote speeches to three day intensive conferences. One of my favorite audience responses came after I delivered a twenty-five minute keynote at the end of a three hour session in a packed auditorium of about 1,200 students. She said, "You were impossible to ignore." My first thought after she said this was, "So, what you are saying is that you were trying to ignore me, but were unsuccessful?" Seriously though, she went on to say that it was one of the most engaging twenty-five minutes she has experienced from a convention keynote speaker and she has seen a good number of us.

This lesson is not about celebrating me, but rather about celebrating the strategies I employ to create engaging keynotes. Following are a few reasons why I think she was unsuccessful at ignoring me.

1. High-Level Interaction. The first half consisted of humor (wit, not jokes), building rapport by telling a quick story about an experience I had that they are currently going through and two quick full-audience interactive activities. There was zero space in the first twelve minutes to be physically, mentally or emotionally disengaged.

2. Clear Outline. The second half was the content. The title of the keynote was The Three Giant Jumps to Have a Giant

Leadership Journey. Everything about the content pieces revolved around the three jumps. This repetition built in anticipation to find out what the three were going to be. This anticipation added to the "impossible to ignore" effect.

3. Emotion-Based Stories. Each of the "Three Giant Jumps" was delivered in story form. If I would have had more than twenty-five minutes, I would have included another full audience interactive activity to support the second point. Because the points were supported with fast paced, interesting, colorful and emotion-based stories, the ignore factor was diminished by the power of the story. Stories have a built-in start, middle, and end. They have easy to understand reference points. If you tell personal or obscure stories they will contain unique details.

4. Energy. Energy is the most pervasive strategy employed by keynote speakers, workshop presenters and teachers in the Can't Ignore Club. Their voice, body and attitude all communicate, "I am excited and interested to be here, even if you aren't. If you aren't, I'm not going to yell at you or push you into getting there, we are going to have so much fun and get so much done on this side of the fence that you will eventually want to jump it yourself."

This energy strategy results in being able to pull the audience up to your level of attention, involvement, excitement, joy, etc. It is very difficult to ignore someone who is fully invested in the moment and is armed with effective strategies to motivate that same level of investment from the audience.

Unplanned Keynote Moments

54

Big MO

Respond positively to distractions.

If you choose to go highly interactive with your keynotes, you better be ready to handle anything and everything that takes you off plan. While delivering a sixty minute keynote in front of three hundred student leaders and adult advisors in New Mexico I had stage art fall off the wall, a girl in the front row laugh uncontrollably for a full three minutes, a mystery explosion in the fourth row that I think was a balloon popping, a microphone signal that dropped out every twelve minutes and what sounded like a herd of water buffaloes stampeding in the room next door. This turned out to be a facility worker pushing a cart full of something. Needless to say, it was one interesting evening. The following tactics will help you the next time something unexpected comes up during your keynotes.

1. Expect them beforehand. Have a mind like water. Don't get caught off guard by having a rigid mind that absolutely has to stay on plan. This will get you in a more pliable mind-set that will be able to remain calm, relaxed and responsive.

2. Trudge through them with a smile on your face and love in your heart. Unless it is someone being disruptive in a harmful manner, smile through the unplanned moments and enjoy them. If you are calm and enjoying the unplanned moments, your audience will be more likely to do the same.

3. Handle it appropriately relative to the distraction's size and context. If it is something small, let it go with maybe a raised eyebrow and a smile. If it something larger (like the girl in the front row who could barely breathe while explosion laughing for three minutes), stop where you were going and deal with the distraction. If it is large, your audience's attention is there anyway and it is pointless for you to go on. Let your personality decide how you handle it, but the default is to have some fun with it in a positive manner.

4. Jump back on track right were you left off. Restart from where you were and act like it never happened. It is amazing how quickly a group can shift attention back and forth if you take them there confidently, smoothly and efficiently.

5. When you do have a good number of unplanned moments, they are taking time away from your original plan. Don't try to cram everything in. It is better to make quick adjustments mid-stream, prioritize your remaining content and let the audience really get the big messages than to have them barely remember all of them because you had to blow through.

6. Above all else, remember everything happens for a reason. Just because you didn't plan for it to happen, does not mean it wasn't supposed to happen. Be like a master surfer; live in the moment, keep your feet underneath you, be ready for anything, have an awesome time and enjoy the ride.

Concentrate Your Room

55

Big MO

Get everyone facing the same direction.

Your audience has a ton of noise going on during training sessions. The learning and retention of your content hinges on a number of factors. One big factor is your willingness and ability to get everyone physically plugged into the session. Concentrating your training room is about controlling the learning environment to produce the greatest chance for success and it is so simple to do. Follow the techniques below. Does it take more time? Yes. Is it worth it? Yes.

There are five big benefits of concentrating your training room. It removes what my speaking peer and mentor Bill Cordes calls "energy gaps" – the comfort space people normally create. It removes distractions; especially when you have a round table set-up. It gets your audience physically engaged in the session. This creates a boost of attention via heightened awareness, blood flow and brain activity. It creates the perfect environment for the Passionate Paul and Hostage Harriet types in your audience to get plugged in. Finally, it encourages growth in your confidence because the audience will be more attentive.

Here are five concentration tactics that will help you achieve those results.

1. Table Work. You roaming the room. Audience seated at round tables facing each other. Unfortunately, most trainers who have a round table set-up just keep the audience members seated like this throughout the entire session. Everyone is facing different directions and many have their back to the trainer. If they are not looking at the trainer, they are facing a table full of distractions. You should keep the audience in Table Work position only when they are doing group work.

2. High Receive. You in one spot. Chairs and audience members at tables, but facing directly toward you. Use high receive to make key points, video presentations, slide presentations and big group discussions. High receive can easily be overused since the audience members remain at their tables. Don't overuse it. The point of any concentration technique is to make a significant directional change in their body language to create a more focused learning environment. If you overuse any one of these techniques, the technique becomes the norm and attention fatigue will set in.

3. Movie Time. You in one spot. Audience members seated in amphitheater style around you. If you are planning a longer group discussion, illustrating a point with a story or teaching from a flipchart, bring the audience forward and have them sit close to each other and close to you.

4. Corner Cram. You in the corner. Audience members seated in corner with you. Same as movie time, only in a corner.

5. Play Time. You and the audience standing in an open area. If you are using an activity or exercise to illustrate a point, get the room set up like you need it by concentrating where the audience is standing as you give the directions. Push the tables and chairs out of the way, get all the audience members standing together in one place, get attention and go for it.

Your Personality Matters

56

Big MO

Be the best of you and a little of them.

Being an authentic communicator requires a firm understanding of who you are and how you are received by others. Your personality is a major factor in both. Let's match the four major personality types and their potential strengths and weaknesses in the area of speaking, training and teaching.

The first key is to know what type you are and understand how it helps you and hurts you as a presenter. The second key is to understand that you have all four personality types in your audience all the time. You also have parts of all four in you, even though one of the four defines and dominates your personality. You need to include elements that speak to each of the four and rely on the elements that work best with your personality most of the time. This is probably one of the most challenging tasks of the authentic presenter; to be the best of yourself and to be empathetic enough of your audience to say, do and show things you know they will enjoy.

Let's dive into the personality types. My company, YourNextSpeaker, in conjunction with TRI Leadership, created a leadership behavior style assessment called ViewPoint. Send an email to *info@yournextspeaker.com* to receive a free copy of the ViewPoint. This instrument is a simple and brief questionnaire that reveals whether you are a Director, an Actor, a Manager, or a Writer. We used the world of movies for the monikers. Here is a brief overview of the four types:

Directors are primarily interested in function. Directors love to be in charge and thrive on getting things done. They like action.

Actors are primarily interested in fun. Actors live to entertain and be entertained. It is all about the experience. They like energy.

Managers are primarily interested in feelings. Managers are people pleasers and work best when the emotional side of the equation is in equilibrium. They like calm.

Writers are primarily interested in facts. Writers love data. They live for proof and are ready to give it if they think it is needed. They like certainty.

If you have ever taken the DISC or True Colors instruments, the following are the close correlations between the three.

ViewPoint	DISC	True Colors
Directors	D	Gold
Actors	I	Orange
Managers	S	Blue
Writers	C	Green

What are the strengths and weaknesses of each personality type when it comes to giving presentations? If you are familiar with the four major types, many of these will be obvious. If you aren't, this review of each type's strengths and weaknesses will get you up to speed.

Directors. They let their confidence do the talking.
Strengths - inspirational, organized, easily commands room
Weaknesses - overbearing, too concerned with perfection, not willing to admit mistakes
Key Word - function
Best Tool - prepared stanzas

Actors. They let the experience do the talking.
Strengths - interaction, high-energy, risk-taker
Weaknesses - too high-strung, all fluff/no meat, going too fast to read audience
Key Word - fun
Best Tool - activities

Managers. They let their personal connection with the audience do the talking.
Strengths - story telling, audience-focused, relaxed
Weaknesses - feelings easily hurt, long winded, all fluff/no meat
Key Word - feelings
Best Tool - group discussion

Writers. They let the data do the talking.
Strengths - supporting data, rational thinking, calm
Weaknesses - perceived as arrogant, information overload, all meat/no fluff
Key Word - facts
Best Tool – slide shows

The big learning lesson here is the most effective presenters have a good mix of quotes, stories, data and activities to speak to all personality types in the room and they rely heavily on the best tools of their authentic style.

This information is also valuable if you are presenting with one or more people. Presenting in pairs can be effective if you understand how the other person is built and know their strengths and weaknesses up front. Take some time to not only discuss your presentation's flow, but to discover what each of you really want to present. One of you might be better suited to lead an activity while the other one is a great storyteller.

Tips for Presenting with a Partner

1. *When you aren't speaking, be a great audience member. Sit with them and do what they are doing.*
2. *Follow the plan you designed unless you both agree to go a different direction mid-presentation.*
3. *Lift up and encourage your partner. Your audience will pick up even subtle positive (or negative) remarks or body language and their trust in your partner (and you) will be impacted.*
4. *During transitions, build on where your partner left off – even if it is just a sentence that serves as a bridge between their content and yours.*
5. *Be totally present in what your partner is doing so you can tell when they need your help.*

Great Speaker Introductions

57

Big MO

The speaker introduction is the speech's start.

The best introductions are short and sweet. Use the following five elements to build your next speaker introduction. Also, do what you can to get the main points of these five in your head and easily accessible. Learn them to the point where you don't have to read the introduction word for word. If you memorize it word for word, practice hard saying it naturally and with authenticity.

1. Say their name correctly. Spell it out phonetically if you have to. Ex., Law-buck, instead of Laubach.

2. Say their current organization and how the work it is doing relates to the audience members.

3. Say their expertise and how it relates to the presentation's focus. This is about their content.

4. Say why this particular speaker is credible. This is about the speaker.

5. Say something unique or interesting about the presenter. This will require you doing some research prior to the day of the program.

Powerful Slide Shows

58

Big MO

Slide shows are for visual support.

Chances are good you give slide show presentations. Chances are even better you are doing it wrong. You are not to blame though. Your peers offer poor examples of how to leverage the power of slide shows. As a professional speaker and executive presentation coach, I have seen slide shows used for good and bad. When used effectively, they are visually stimulating, communicate only the most important points and make complicated ideas more digestible. When used poorly they are distracting crutches that actually diminish the audience's retention of ideas and concepts. Poorly built slide shows are information heavy and wordy.

The key is to take the focus off the screen and place it on the connection between you and your audience. All presentations are emotional at some level. Therefore, your goal as a presenter is to transfer emotion. Even highly technical presentations aren't about the numbers alone. They are about either how you feel about the numbers or what you are or aren't going to do about the numbers.

Slide shows should be used only when you need to add visual support to your presentation. Use images that fill the entire screen. Never use clip art. If you need to put text on the screen also, use images that have a quiet space where you can put the text. You can purchase high quality images for as cheap as one dollar per image on-line. My favorite site is *istockphoto.com.*

There are a few small, but powerful design guidelines you need to follow to keep your slide shows attractive and beneficial to your message. Fonts should be simple and at least thirty point. Never use more than twenty words per slide. You should never read the text on the screen. If you have to use bullet points, you know you are putting too much information on the screen. Try to use less than fifteen slides. If you are using a slide transition, use the simple and classy fade option. All the other ones only distract. Use dark backgrounds and light text or vice-versa and never use red or yellow text.

Finally, if you are going to give out hard copies of your slides to the audience, wait until the end of your presentation. If you pass them out before or during, they will only distract the audience from focusing on you and the screen.

Perfect Banquet Talks

59

Big MO

Be entertaining.

Our final chapter is the shortest and it is about your banquet talks. Banquets are primarily for entertainment purposes; socializing, awarding, recognizing, etc. You should embrace this reality and not bore the audience with your vitally important information. The recipe for great banquets talks is simple.

1. Use only 80% of the allotted time.

2. 80% of your content is entertaining and engaging.

3. 20% of your content is informative or instructional.

Follow this and they will love you.

WHAT DID I LEARN?

Capture the key leadership lessons from this section. Be specific about application and results. Where will you apply the lessons and what are the benefits of growing in those areas?

APPENDIX

The Big MOs

SECTION 1 – GET YOURSELF IN GEAR

1. Every useful brush has a canvas to leave its mark.
2. If you can't be excellent at it, don't be it at all.
3. High performers are in love with their craft.
4. Keeping fuel tanks full protects healthy stress.
5. Give praise, build others and serve the greater good.
6. People give their time to what is really important to them.
7. Challenging goals are growth food.
8. Push the boundaries.
9. Make time for Epic Journeys.
10. Attach a strong positive anchor to the truth.
11. Cool ideas are made from elbow grease.
12. Focus on the cause, not the conditions.
13. Success is determined by what you do with failure.
14. Epic goals get done by forgetting how to give up.
15. Big impact comes from small, mundane acts.
16. Listen and ask open-ended questions.
17. Be clear and loud with your affiliations.
18. Your digital footprint leaves a lasting impression.

SECTION 2 – GET YOUR TEAM IN GEAR

19. Individuals, not teams, do things.
10. People remember how you made them feel.
21. Foster healthy relationships.
22. Decide what an amazing job looks like.
23. Treat others like they want to be treated.
24. Use care-isma.
25. Deal with the relationship first.
26. Build trust across all relationship levels.
27. Fully listening is rare.
28. People need to be inspired to give their best.

29. Begin by looking for the good.
30. Ask questions to strengthen trust.
31. A big challenge must have a big purpose.
32. Negative people need evidence to change.
33. Controlling leaders lead from fear.
34. The medium is as important as the message.
35. The loudest people do not always have the best ideas.
36. Be prepared for a no, but fight for a yes.
37. Take control or the meeting will control you.

SECTION 3 – GET YOUR PRESENTATIONS IN GEAR

38. Give concrete, visual, simple messages.
39. Credibility starts with authenticity.
40. Give your talks zest, flavor and life.
41. Less information is more.
42. Know your stuff top to bottom.
43. Broken time rules kill presentations.
44. Quickly figure out your unique position.
45. Smile and express genuine charisma.
46. Get everyone engaged to improve output.
47. Your presentation starts before you do.
48. Orchestrate their involvement.
49. An auditorium's cons can be pros.
50. Use emotions to get and keep attention.
51. Once you lose control, you lose trust.
52. Response always has a reason.
53. Be fully engaged.
54. Respond positively to distractions.
55. Get everyone facing the same direction.
56. Be the best of you and a little of them.
57. The speaker introduction is the speech's start.
58. Slide shows are for visual support.
59. Be entertaining.

The PLI Curriculum

Personal
Leadership
Insight

The PLI curriculum is a product of a combined 30 years of leadership teaching and training experience. The Personal Leadership Insight curriculum was co-developed by Rhett Laubach and Ryan Underwood as a turn-key system for teaching and learning leadership.   The curriculum is built on the foundation of the ten PLI Essentials: Vision, Integrity, Innovativeness, Wise Judgement, Service Mindedness, Goal Processing, Skill Assessment, Emotional Maturity, Fostering Relationships and Masterful Communication.

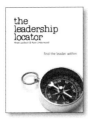

The Leadership Locator. This interactive, spiral-bound student workbook is both visually pleasing and full of new leadership study material. It works for both personal leadership development study, as well as class study time. The Leadership Locator guides the students through the ten PLI Essentials and provides challenges and tools for developing their leadership potential. *($24.95 each. Set of 30 - $600)*

The Navigator. The teacher's guidebook contains strategies for teaching the Leadership Locator, it also contains 50 leadership exercises with step-by-step instructions and 10 Ventures that gives the students a chance to put their leadership to the test. This 200-page leadership training system is three-hole punched for ease of use and flexibility. *($74.95 each)*

The PLI Primer. A shorter version of the Leadership Locator, the PLI Primer is a great way to get your feet wet. It comes in booklet form (11 x17 folded in half, stapled spine) and contains the basic content necessary to learn about each of the PLI Essentials.
($9.95 each)

The PLI Website. Whether you teach the full PLI curriculum or not, the PLI website should be bookmarked as one of your leadership material favorites. It is not only the place to preview and purchase the PLI curriculum, but it is also the place to access literally hours upon hours of no-cost leadership teaching/training resources through the Warehouse and the PLI Blog.
(Absolutely Free)

The PLI iPhone App. Go mobile with PLI curriculum updates and PLI blog posts with our new iPhone App. Just search "PLI Blog" in the iTunes store, download and install. This is the best way to stay current with everything PLI.
(Absolutely Free)

Leadership Library

The following list contains my favorite leadership and presentation books.

1. The Art of Innovation, Tom Kelley
2. The Bible
3. Brain Rules, John Medina
4. The Dip, Seth Godin
5. The Effective Executive, Peter Drucker
6. The Element, Sir Ken Robinson
7. Emotional Intelligence, Daniel Goleman
8. Getting Things Done, David Allen
9. How to Become a Rainmaker, Jeffrey Fox
10. How to Say it for Women, Phyllis Mindell
11. How to Win Friends and Influence People, Dale Carnegie
12. Influence, Robert Cialdini
13. Inspire any Audience, Tony Jeary
14. Leadership 101, John Maxwell
15. Leadership is an Art, Max DePree
16. Little Black Book of Connections, Jeffrey Gitomer
17. Made to Stick, Chip and Dan Heath
18. Now, Discover Your Strengths, Marcus Buckingham
19. Presentation Zen, Garr Reynolds
20. Quantum Teaching, Bobbi DePorter
21. Season of Life, Jeffrey Marz
22. See You at the Top, Zig Ziglar
23. Seven Habits of Highly Effective People, Stephen Covey
24. Slide:ology, Nancy Duarte
25. The Story Factor, Annette Simmons
26. Teaching as Leadership, Steven Farr
27. Three Signs of a Miserable Job, Patrick Lencioni
28. Think and Grow Rich, Napoleon Hill
29. The Tipping Point, Malcolm Gladwell
30. Winning with People, John Maxwell

Blog Library

The following list contains my favorite leadership and presentation blogs.

1. Books – *blog.800ceoread.com*
2. Brain Science – *brainrules.blogspot.com*
3. Business & Sales – *www.thejfblogit.co.uk*
4. Happiness – *www.happiness-project.com*
5. Ideas – *ben.casnocha.com*
6. Ideas – *changethis.com/blog*
7. Ideas – *sethgodin.typepad.com*
8. Ideas – *www.danpink.com*
9. Leadership – *plileadership.blogspot.com**
10. Leadership - *blogs.hbr.org/goldsmith*
11. Leadership – *www.allthingsworkplace.com*
12. Leadership – *www.leadershipnow.com/leadingblog*
13. Leadership – *www.marksanborn.com/blog*
14. Presentation Design – *blog.duarte.com*
15. Presentation Design – *www.ethos3.com/blog*
16. Presentation Design – *www.presentationzen.com*
17. Presenting – *www.AuthenticityRules.com**
18. Presenting – *sixminutes.dlugan.com*
19. Productivity – *www.zenhabits.com*
20. Productivity – *www.marcandangel.com*

* *Rhett's blog*

NOTES

NOTES

NOTES

NOTES

NOTES